THE HAMLYN BOOK OF

TROPICAL FRESHWATER FISH

David Alderton

HAMLYN

The Hamlyn Book of Tropical Freshwater Fish
David Alderton

First published in 1997 by
Hamlyn
an imprint of Reed International Books Ltd
Michelin House, 81 Fulham Road, London, SW3 6RB
and Auckland, Melbourne, Singapore and Toronto

Publishing Director **Laura Bamford**

Executive Editor **Simon Tuite**
Project Editor **Katie Cowan**
Editor **Dawn Marie Gratton Stephenson**

Art Director **Keith Martin**
Executive Art Editor **Mark Stevens**
Art Editor **Lisa Tai**
Illustration **Line and Line**
Picture Researcher **Emily Hedges**
Photographers **Paul Forrester and Colin Bowling**

Production **Josephine Allum**

British Library Cataloguing-in-Publication Data
A catalogue record for this book is available from the British Library

ISBN 0 600 59151 4

Typset in Rotis San Serif

Produced by Mandarin Offset
Printed and bound in China

CONTENTS

INTRODUCTION

There are few hobbies as relaxing as keeping tropical fish. It is no coincidence that in potentially stressful situations, such as a dentist's waiting room, there is often an aquarium. Scientific investigations have shown how simply watching fish can serve to lower blood pressure and help to provide an antidote to the stresses of modern life.

Setting up an aquarium has never been easier thanks to the reliability of modern equipment, while a host of prepared foods and other accessories make the care of the fish quite straightforward. An attractive aquarium offers an absorbing view of the natural world, but it is possible to expand your interest still further. You may want to breed your fish, for example, and this will offer an additional fascinating insight into their behaviour.

Tropical fish are farmed on a huge scale in many countries around the world and colour variants are now established in a number of species. Alterations to the shape of the fins have also arisen in many of the more free-breeding species such as guppies. These variations represent a field of considerable scope for genetic studies.

There are also plenty of opportunities to contact fellow enthusiasts. Various aquatic societies exist for those with an interest in a particular group of fish, such as cichlids. These organisations produce regular bulletins updating members on the latest information in the field; on a local level, clubs sometimes organize shows for their members. In addition, there are bulletin boards and similar information points available on the Internet.

SCIENTIFIC NAMING OF FISH

One of the most difficult and controversial areas of fishkeeping is the scientific naming of the fish. Authors may use different names for the same species and this can create practical problems for fishkeepers interested in finding out more about their fish.

The scientific name of a fish comprises two or three parts. In the case of the five-banded barb, for example, the first part of the scientific name shows the genus to which it belongs–*Barbus* in this case. The species is identified by adding a further description after the genus name; in this case, the result would be *Barbus pentazona*. In some instances the species can be further split into subspecies by the addition of a third term, as in *Barbus pentazona pentazona* and *Barbus pentazona hexazona*.

Unfortunately, the generic name may vary at times to the extent that the five-banded barb has also been classified under the scientific names of *Barbodes pentazona* and *Puntius pentazona*. Therefore, when using an index or searching for a fish it may be necessary to use just the second part of the species' name–*pentazona* in this case–in order to be sure that you have not overlooked it.

Hopefully, as DNA classification becomes more widely applied, many of these taxonomic arguments will become irrelevant. At present, classification tends to be based on physical similarities, such as scale counts, rather than on evidence of a close genetic relationship between particular fish, which provides a much more objective assessment.

THE MEANING OF pH

Water chemistry plays an important part in the care of fish. While some fish are highly adaptable, others have very specific requirements. There are two indicators which are especially significant in this respect–the pH reading and the relative hardness of the water. Both should be measured regularly by means of test kits or by meters, which are more costly.

The pH figure represents the relative acidity or alkalinity of the water; a reading of 7.0 is neutral. It describes the concentration of hydrogen ions in the water relative to the hydroxyl ions; a high pH reading therefore indicates a more dilute concentration of hydrogen ions in the water and alkaline water conditions, whereas a low pH reading reflects acidic conditions with a greater number of hydrogen ions present.

In a particular area the pH reading will be influenced by a number of factors, such as the rocks through which the water has filtered. For example, if it has originated from bore holes in chalk, then the chalk will have made it more alkaline.

Once the water is in the aquarium, other factors will become significant. The substrate and the decor may have an effect on the pH value. Limestone gravel or rocks, for example, will have the same effect as chalk. However, as the fish's waste is broken down the water will become more acidic. There are also substances called buffers, notably sodium bicarbonate, which are usually present in the water and serve to curtail dramatic swings in pH.

Freshwater fish generally have adapted to live within a pH range of 5–9.5, with adult fish being more adaptable than fry. Rapid alterations in pH should be avoided and partial water changes will effectively dilute the build-up of nitric acid produced by biological filtration, which causes the progressive acidification of the water.

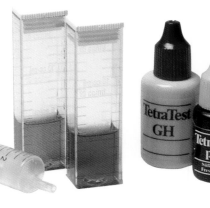

Test kits are required for checking the local water chemistry and monitoring the water in the aquarium.

Test meters are being used increasingly in the aquarium hobby as an easy means of obtaining the pH of a sample of water.

Adding peat to the filter will create an acidic environment for those fish that require it, but peat also depresses the activity of the bacteria involved in biological filtration. These bacteria function most effectively around pH 7.0 and it may therefore be necessary to take other steps, such as the use of zeolite which absorbs ammonia directly, to maintain the water quality.

In the case of fish which live in alkaline surroundings, a limestone substrate and rocks are beneficial, as suggested earlier. Fish from such environments are less able to adapt to changes in pH than those which live under acidic conditions. Periodic additions of fresh sources of limestone to aquaria of this type will therefore be needed because as the limestone dissolves its buffering capacity is lost and the pH is likely to fall accordingly.

UNDERSTANDING WATER HARDNESS

This is a measure of the dissolved salts present in the water. In hard water areas kettles will gain a coating of fur, resulting from the deposition of carbonates caused by boiling. The presence of carbonates is responsible for temporary hardness (often abbreviated as KH) and is linked to pH, because bicarbonate salts in the water are basically responsible both for temporary hardness and alkalinity. In contrast, total hardness (GH) is a reflection of both temporary and permanent hardness.

Various systems exist for measuring the hardness of water, but the degrees dH scale is the most widely used internationally. This system is in turn linked to the number of milligrammes of calcium carbonate per litre of water. One degree dH is equivalent to 17.9mg/l of calcium carbonate, with a reading of 3 degrees dH being considered soft, while a reading in excess of 25 degrees dH indicates very hard water.

It is possible to adjust temporary hardness by using limestone to make the water harder, or diluting with distilled water so it becomes softer. Special ion exchange resins are another, more costly, means of softening tap water for the aquarium. Fish from the Amazon basin are accustomed to soft water conditions, whereas those from the Rift Valley of Africa live in hard water surroundings. When planning a community aquarium, it is therefore important to ensure that the fish which you are choosing are compatible in terms of their water chemistry requirements.

EXPLAINING THE SYMBOLS

The distribution maps give an idea of where in the world a particular fish occurs. A few of the species in this book are found in the USA, and these are included in the Central America distribution. More precise distribution information can be found in the entries themselves.

The feeding preference of the fish shows the favoured diet, but this is not to say that in a community aquarium, for example, a fish which is primarily herbivorous will not occasionally eat worms. Variety in the diet is important and experimentation within reason is recommended.

Individual fish do differ in terms of their behaviour but signs of aggression are most likely to emerge as the time for spawning approaches. Other factors, such as the degree of cover in the aquarium, may also influence this type of behaviour.

Species tagged as being anti-social are likely to be both aggressive and predatory, although most fish will eat small fry if an opportunity presents itself. The label 'may be aggressive' indicates a pugnacious nature which is often displayed towards other members of their own kind.

'Social' is also a relative term, which should take into account the size of the fish; as a general rule, it is not a good idea to combine fish of widely differing sizes. Smaller fish are likely to become stressed under these circumstances, particularly within the confines of a fairly small tank, even if they are not directly harassed. The figure for size gives an indication of how large a species may grow in aquarium surroundings, although it is not uncommon to find growth variations under these conditions.

KEY TO SYMBOLS

DISTRIBUTION MAP

Africa

Asia

Australia

Central America

South America

SIZE
(to nearest inch/½ cm)

00in 00cm

WATER pH

Acidic

Acid – neutral

Neutral

Alkaline – neutral

Alkaline

FEEDING

Carnivore

Omnivore

Herbivore

HABIT

Anti-social

May be aggressive

Social

TANK LEVEL

All levels

Bottom level

Mid-level down

Mid-level

Mid-level up

Top level

WATER HARDNESS

Hard water

Medium-hard water

Medium water

Medium-soft water

Soft water

Setting up the Aquarium

You will need to decide on the type of fish which you are intending to keep at an early stage so that you can plan the aquarium accordingly. Today's tanks are generally made of sheets of glass anchored together by special silicone sealant, which absorbs the pressure of the water.

The size of the tank will have a direct bearing on the total number of fish you can keep. As a guide, you should allow about 1in of fish per imperial gallon of water (approximately 1cm per 2 litres). It will be easier to work in metric dimensions for this purpose, since you can simply multiply the height, length and width dimensions of the tank together in centimetres and divide by 1000 to give the volume in litres.

Acrylic tanks are relatively small in size and, although useful for isolation or spawning purposes, they are not generally large enough for a community aquarium. The surface of these tanks can be damaged quite easily and algae may colonize the resulting scratches, detracting from the aquarium, so cleaning has to be carried out with particular care.

The likely adult size of the fish you are seeking is also significant when selecting an aquarium. It is easier and cheaper to set up a relatively large unit from the outset, rather than having to change repeatedly as the fish grow bigger. While it is the length of the aquarium that is the figure most often considered, the width and height are of equal significance for the comfort of the fish. Tall fish, such as the angelfish, need correspondingly deeper aquaria, averaging 18in (46cm) deep, and they must be able to turn round without difficulty, so the width of the tank is equally important.

POSITIONING THE AQUARIUM

Deciding on the location of the aquarium in the room is important, because once the tank is set up it will be impossible to move it without dismantling it again. Choose a locality away from bright sunlight, because this is likely to result in fluctuations in the temperature of the water and will soon cause the sides of the tank to be covered with unsightly algae. Avoid locating the aquarium near a radiator, which will alter the water temperature.

Fish are very sensitive to vibration and they should not be kept close to a door which is regularly opened and shut. Equally, the aquarium should not be sited near to a television or hi-fi system, partly because of the risk of any water spillage damaging this equipment. When setting up an aquarium, you may want to check that your household insurance policy covers you for accidental damage, just in case there is any leakage in the future.

Easy access to a power point is also an important consideration because of the danger of trailing electrical flexes around the room. It should be possible to run the power supply to any electrical equipment via a junction box, in the form of a cable tidy, rather than using adaptors at the

POSITIONING THE AQUARIUM

Easy access to a power point is important, because of the danger of trailing electrical flexes around the room and the need to switch off and disconnect the power on occasions.

Avoid locating the aquarium near a radiator, which will alter the water temperature and could cause it to rise to a fatal level.

Choose a locality away from bright sunlight, because this is also likely to result in fluctuations in the temperature of the water and will soon cause the sides of the tank to be covered with unsightly algae.

Fish are very sensitive to vibration and they should not be kept close to a door which is regularly opened and shut.

The aquarium should not be sited near to a television or hi-fi system, because of the sound from such sources.

Keep the aquarium away from electrical equipment, because of the risk of any water spillage damaging it.

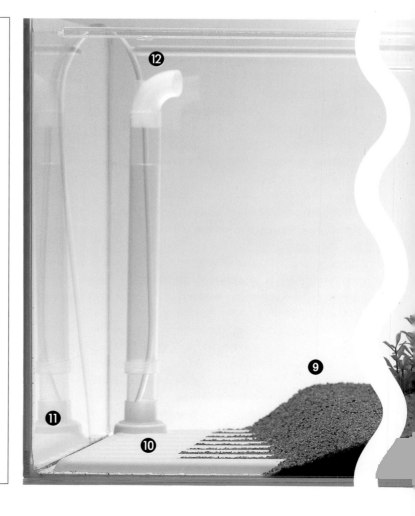

power point. Using a cable tidy is a much safer option, partly because of the fact that the electrical equipment, with the exception of the lighting, will need to be left running constantly.

A secure base for the aquarium is vital, since a gallon of water weighs in excess of 8lb (1litre weighs 0.8kg), and the weight of a fairly standard aquarium, measuring 36in long x 12in wide and 15in high (91cm x 30cm x 38cm), will be 230lb (104kg). It is possible to purchase an aquarium set in a cabinet as a piece of furniture for the room or, alternatively, a separate stand may be chosen. Even if you decide to place the aquarium on a stout cabinet in the room, be sure to fit a polystyrene base between the base of the tank and its support. This is critical, as the polystyrene will absorb any unevenness in the surface which might otherwise exert undue pressure on part of the base of the aquarium, causing a leak.

Decorative sheets which fit externally on to the glass at the rear of the aquarium are becoming increasingly popular, as they help to convey a feeling of depth and block any unsightly background. It is much easier to fit them before the tank is in position.

CHOOSING THE SUBSTRATE

Gravel is the most widely used material for covering the aquarium floor. Although there are various colour options they can look rather artificial, with red gravel, for example, definitely detracting from the appearance of fish of this colour in the water above. The amount of gravel that will be required to provide a suitable depth on the floor of the aquarium can be calculated on the basis of approximately 2lb per gallon (1kg per 4.5 litres). The final depth should be about 3in (7.5cm).

Place the gravel in a colander and wash it thoroughly under a running tap. In order to be sure of killing possible disease-causing organisms, transfer the gravel to a bucket of water containing a suitable aquarium disinfectant.

Most aquaria contain an under-gravel filter, which consists of a plastic corrugated plate with holes or slits placed on the floor of the aquarium. The gravel is

Aquarium gravel is available in a range of sizes and colours. Always wash it very thoroughly to prevent a scum forming on the water.

Features of a typical aquarium

1 Tall plants set towards the rear of the tank
2 Thermometer to check the water temperature
3 Filter uplift tube attached to the under-gravel filter returns clean, aerated water to the tank
4 Polystyrene sheet under tank
5 Hollow decor provides retreats for some fish
6 Combined heaterstat unit with suckers
7 Small plants set in clumps in foreground
8 Rockwork or substitutes provide potential spawning sites
9 Well-washed gravel
10 Under-gravel filter plate buried under gravel
11 Glass held in place by special sealant
12 Airline connected to air pump out of the tank

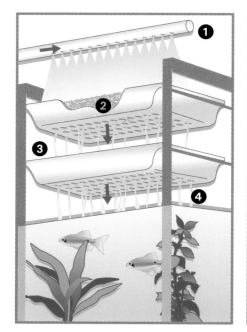

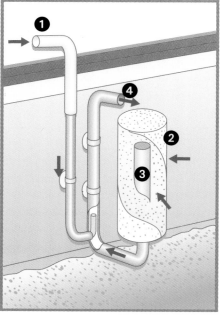

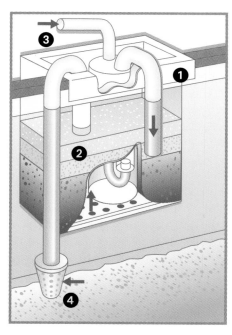

Trickle filter

1 Water flows out of spray bar

2 Partially submerged filter wool

3 Water exposed to oxygen in the air

4 Trickles through plates back to the aquarium

Sponge filter

1 Attachment to air pump

2 Sponge which acts as a filter medium

3 Central plastic core to the filter

4 Water leaves with higher oxygen content

External box filter

1 Lip holds filter to the outside of the tank

2 Filter media arranged in layers in the box

3 Attachment to air pump

4 Water intake from aquarium

then placed on top and ultimately acts as a filter bed. Beneficial bacteria in the gravel break down waste in the aquarium water as it passes through the filter bed. The gravel needs to be reasonably coarse, comprising particles approximately 0.13in (3–4mm) in size, or this type of filter will not be able to function effectively.

Sand is sometimes chosen as a substrate but is less suitable than gravel in this respect and, in such aquaria, greater reliance will have to be placed on alternative filtration systems. Fish which originate from hard water areas will benefit from the use of limestone chips to form the lining on the aquarium base.

DECORATING THE AQUARIUM

Rockwork in the aquarium helps to provide cover for the fish, and potential spawning sites in some cases, as well as enhancing its appearance. Supplies of suitable smooth rocks are usually available from aquarist stores. These rocks represent a safe option compared with rocks from other sources, which could be harmful to the fish either because they are contaminated with chemicals or because they might dissolve in the water, affecting the water chemistry as a result. Calciferous rocks, for example, must only be included

in aquaria where hard water conditions are needed.

Rocks should be washed thoroughly with an aquarium disinfectant and securely positioned alongside the rest of the tank decor; they are heavy and must not be balanced loosely on each other as they could collapse or even be dislodged by large fish. If necessary, pieces of rock can be stuck together with aquarium sealant to form cave-like structures, with new clay flowerpots being used as cave linings or simply buried in the substrate.

Bogwood is also commercially available for aquaria use, but it requires more preparation than rockwork. Bogwood contains tannins which can be beneficial in some aquaria, such as those including tetras, but which turn the water brown at first. Soaking the bogwood in water that is changed regularly can reduce this problem by leaching some of the tannins out of the wood. The alternative to soaking is to varnish the wood thoroughly, effectively sealing the surfaces, although the varnish is likely to be toxic if any fish eat it. It may therefore be better to purchase artificial wood, which is basically indistinguishable from the real thing, especially in aquaria where tannic water conditions are not required.

HEATING AND FILTRATION

The tank decor should be used to disguise equipment such as the uplift for the under-gravel filter. The heaterstat can also be concealed, but it is important to ensure that there is an adequate flow of water around here so that the heat is evenly distributed. Heaterstats are available in a range of sizes and wattages; most are pre-set to 77°F (25°C), although they can be easily adjusted if required. Allow about 100 watts of power per 22 gallons (100 litres) of water. These devices generally last for at least three years but it is best to choose one of the designs which switch off automatically if there is a risk of overheating, to safeguard the fish.

Some large fish will attack heaterstats in their quarters, with potentially fatal consequences. It is safer with such individuals to heat the water in the aquarium by means of a thin pad placed outside the tank, under separate thermostatic control. These pads are available in a range of different sizes.

Accurate monitoring of the temperature can be achieved with a thermometer. External digital designs are preferred these days, but the colours can attract young fingers and this may lead to distorted readings. An alarm to warn you of heating

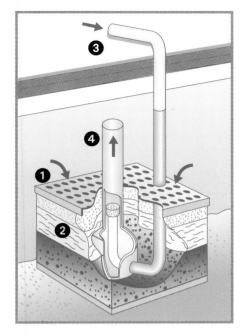

Internal box filter
1 *Lid of filter perforated to provide inlet*
2 *Water drawn down through layers in filter*
3 *Attachment to air pump*
4 *Vertical return pipe*

failure is another possible safety feature.

A wide range of filters can now be obtained. Power filters contain both a motor, to draw the water through the system, and a filter unit, which may consist of just a simple foam cartridge populated by beneficial bacteria or an elaborate mixture of items. Activated carbon may typically be added to a filter because of its ability to absorb waste products, while peat will serve to acidify the water.

Check on the cost of these disposable components for filters because they can add considerably to the running expenses of the aquarium, when a cheaper option could prove to be just as satisfactory. Some power filters–typically those with larger capacities–are external and can be fitted behind the aquarium out of sight, whereas internal models have to be located in the tank itself. Both filter models help to ensure that there is good circulation of the water in the aquarium.

An air pump will be needed to operate the under-gravel filter. Choose a quiet model and place it on a smooth surface which will discourage any vibration. The pump must never be covered in any way. A non-return valve to prevent back flow of water into this unit is also essential, located near the outlet from the pump.

Aquarium Plants

The inclusion of living plants will help to create an attractive natural aquascape and improve the aquarium environment.

PLANTS AND PHOTOSYNTHESIS
During the hours of daylight, plants utilize carbon dioxide present in the water. This gas, combined with light, is vital for the manufacture of carbohydrates, providing nutrients for the plants. The process is known as photosynthesis. Tiny bubbles can often be seen coming off the plants in a well-lit aquarium; this is oxygen being released back by the plant. At night however, the situation is reversed, with the plants and fish both utilizing oxygen and producing carbon dioxide.

In an aquarium without plants, or with plastic substitutes, photosynthesis cannot take place. Plants are advantageous because they use both the carbon dioxide and nitrates resulting from the breakdown of the waste produced by the fish, and so have a beneficial biological effect in the environment. In addition, they use the nitrate resulting from the breakdown of the fish's waste as a fertilizer. Aquaria are far more likely to be blighted by the growth of unsightly algae if they do include living plants, because these microscopic plants face no competition for nutrients here.

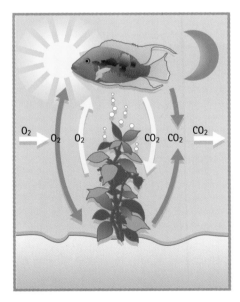

Photosynthesis is the process by which plants use daylight and carbon dioxide (CO_2) to make their nutrients. Additional oxygen (O_2) is released back into the aquarium as a by-product. At night, however, the situation is reversed.

There may be circumstances, however, where certain living plants cannot be included, often because they may be uprooted by the fish. It might be possible to choose plants which grow on rocks or other tank decor though, as well as floating plants on the surface of the water.

Put aquatic plants back into water as soon as possible after purchase, washing them first in a solution containing an aquarium disinfectant to avoid introducing any diseases to the tank. Careful planning is important, so that there will be no need to disturb the plants as they grow.

Taller plants should be situated at the back and around the sides of the tank, with one being used as a centrepiece. By setting plants in pots, there is less risk of their roots blocking the slits of the under-gravel filter. These pots can then be concealed by gravel.

Smaller plants can occupy the foreground and some can be affixed to the tank decor. Although little subsequent care is generally needed, proper lighting conditions will be essential if the plants are to thrive for any length of time in the aquarium. Floating plants provide cover, and are especially appreciated by fish which live close to the surface. They may also be used as a spawning site in some cases.

As an alternative for large fish which are destructive towards vegetation, it is now possible to purchase very realistic plastic plants. These can simply be weighed down and buried in the gravel.

LIGHTING
Living plants need adequate lighting if they are to grow in the aquarium. Using daylight for this purpose is not practical because the level of illumination in the room may be low, while placing the aquarium in front of a window is likely to lead to overheating with fatal consequences during the summer.

The most satisfactory way of providing light under these circumstances is to use specially designed fluorescent tubes. Some tubes, notably those emitting light from the blue end of the spectrum, may be better for plant growth than for bringing out the natural coloration of the fish, so you may have to decide accordingly if you are relying on a single tube.

As a general guide, choose a tube which is just shorter than the length of the aquarium; for brighter illumination, tubes of the same wattage can be used in pairs. This is particularly important in the case of deeper tanks, where the light output may otherwise not penetrate satisfactorily down to the lower levels. You must be careful however not to raise the temperature at the water's surface; this applies especially in breeding set-ups where there may be a bubble nest or where fish are confined in a breeding trap. While fluorescent tubes have a comparatively low heat output, spotlights of any kind are particularly problematic in this respect.

The lights will need to be fitted in the hood over the aquarium–safety is paramount. Use special fitments which are damp resistant and be sure that the tubes are screened from the water. Lighting should be restricted to a maximum of 12 hours a day and will need to be reduced if algal growth starts to become a problem.

You can check whether the plants are receiving enough light to grow by using a special probe and light meter. This will also reveal when the light output from the tubes is declining to the stage where they will need replacing. Most tubes are likely to last about a year under average conditions.

SNAILS

The inclusion of snails in an aquarium is not always recommended, firstly because they could eat the plants and secondly because some fish will prey upon them. Nevertheless, snails can add an extra focus of interest and even help to keep algal growth in check. One of the most popular varieties is the golden apple snail (*Pomacea bridgesi*), which originated from South America and grows to a length of about 2in (5cm). It is actually a colour morph of a much duller, greenish-brown snail.

If you decide to add snails, be prepared to keep their numbers in check. This is done most easily by removing their jelly-like spawn before it can hatch. It is always worthwhile checking aquatic plants prior to planting them in the aquarium as they may already have eggs laid on them, which could give rise to an unexpected explosion of young snails. Snails are hermaphrodite, which means that they have both sexes present in their bodies, and keeping two snails together will inevitably result in fertile eggs being produced.

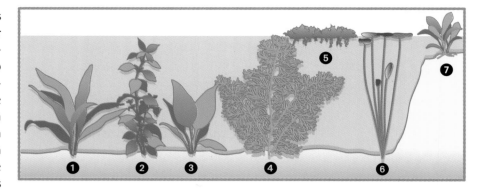

Aquarium plants come in many different forms and have varying growth patterns. A number of them do not grow totally submerged throughout the year in their native habitat, with the result that they will not thrive for long and often grow more slowly in aquarium surroundings.

Types of aquatic plants
1 strap-like leaves; 2 coarse leaves;
3 broad leaves; 4 fine leaves;
5 floating plant; 6 surface-growing leaves;
7 leaves above the surface

When filling the tank, avoid disturbing the gravel by placing a plate on top and pouring the water over it. Keep a check that the temperature is not too hot.

Set the plants in place once the tank is partially full and the water is roughly at the right temperature. You can buy plants individually or as collections for aquaria of different sizes.

Apple snails can live for a couple of years under favourable conditions, but take care if you are treating the aquarium with any medication for the fish as this could harm the snails. Snail eggs take three months or so to hatch.

The finished aquarium. Note the use of specimen plants in the front of the tank and how plants are grouped together in clumps. Roots are of little significance to aquatic plants, although they will help to anchor them in place. When purchasing plants, avoid any which look yellowed or damaged. Be sure to keep them moist by placing them in a bucket of water until they can be planted; leaving them in the air will damage their leaves.

FOREGROUND PLANTS

Java moss *Vesicularia dubyana*
LIGHT REQUIREMENT : low
TEMPERATURE : 72–77°F (22–25°C)
SUBSTRATE : submerged wood, rocks
pH READING : neutral
WATER : soft

This plant originates from south-eastern Asia, ranging from parts of India eastwards, including the island of Java, with over 130 different species present in Asia and Africa. There can sometimes be problems over identification and only a few species are truly aquatic. True Java moss will grow either in an underwater setting, or it can be allowed to grow above the water level. The

plant grows quite slowly, but its dense growth provides a safe spawning ground for egg laying species and also offers a retreat for young fry. It can be held in position on a piece of bogwood, for example, by means of a rubber band until it has established itself.

Although Java moss prefers soft water, it is very adaptable in terms of its growing requirements. It is not a good idea to include it in a brightly lit part of the aquarium because algae may swamp its growth, developing within the dense fronds. The only thing to do under these circumstances is to discard the plant and start again. Propagation is easy–just break off pieces from the clump.

Dwarf cryp *Cryptocoryne nevillii*
LIGHT REQUIREMENT : bright
TEMPERATURE : 68–77°F (20–25°C)
SUBSTRATE : gravel
pH READING : neutral
WATER : soft

This small member of the *Cryptocoryne* genus occurs naturally on the island of Sri Lanka. It measures up to 4in (10cm) in height and has distinctive bright-green, lance-like leaves on stalks. It is a good idea to pot these plants in shallow containers filled with fine grade gravel, compared with that used on the floor of the tank, as they tend to grow better this way.

Growth may be slow at first but in well-lit surroundings these plants will develop well. In due course, you can divide the plants or split off runners and use these to establish further plants. The runners will produce side shoots more rapidly and in greater numbers if they are left loose in the aquarium at first.

Pygmy chain sword plant *Echinodorus tenellus*
LIGHT REQUIREMENT : shade
TEMPERATURE : 68–77°F (20–25°C)
SUBSTRATE : gravel
pH READING : neutral
WATER : soft

This plant has two separate areas of distribution, in the USA from Michigan to Florida, and in South America where it ranges from Colombia down to southern parts

of Brazil. It has long been popular as an aquarium plant, being easy to cultivate in these surroundings.

There can be variations in size between the different types. In general, pygmy chain sword plants grow to no more than 2–3in (5–7.5cm) in height, although where they are crowded their pattern of growth is more upright so they appear taller.

As a result, it is best to space out the plants in the foreground at the beginning so as to create an attractive, low growing and bright-green array of vegetation. Pygmy chain sword plants dislike hard water and this makes them ideally suited to an Amazonian tank featuring fish such as

cardinal tetras (see page 43).

In order to ensure healthy growth, position the pygmy chain sword plants so that they are protected from bright aquarium light, and in an area where mulm will not accumulate on their leaves. They will not thrive in hot water conditions, so avoid a site near the heater if possible.

Pygmy chain sword plants reproduce by means of stolons or 'runners' which grow out from the base of the plant. As well as being submerged, they can be allowed to break the water's surface, in a spawning tank set-up for example, and they are then likely to produce a mass of tiny white flowers, followed by seeds.

MID-GROUND PLANTS

Banana plant *Nymphoides aquatica*

LIGHT REQUIREMENT : bright

TEMPERATURE : 68–79°F (20–26°C)

SUBSTRATE : gravel

pH READING : neutral

WATER : slightly hard

Some aquatic plants merge into the background, but the banana plant is one which rarely fails to attract attention because of its unusual appearance. This species originates from southern parts of the USA, and has swollen tubercles resembling bananas close to its roots. These tubercles ensure that the plants will not dessicate and die if the water level falls in their natural habitat and exposes the plant's roots.

The leaves of the banana plant usually extend up to the water's surface and provide shade there–although they will prevent light extending down into the lower reaches of the tank, which could be unhelpful in some cases. This plant grows to a height of about 12in (30cm) and is therefore ideal for most tanks.

Flowering can also be achieved in these surroundings with the small white flowers being carried above the water's surface. Propagation can be carried out quite easily by dividing the rootstock or by taking off runners once they have reached a reasonable size, rather than by relying on seed.

African tiger lotus *Nymphaea maculata*

LIGHT REQUIREMENT : bright

TEMPERATURE : 68–86°F (20–30°C)

SUBSTRATE : gravel

pH READING : neutral

WATER : slightly hard

Most aquarium plants are green but there are exceptions, such as this magnificent tiger lotus with its brownish, red and purple hues. It can form a spectacular centrepiece in an aquarium, with the additional benefit that it is undemanding in terms of water chemistry. The leaves can grow to 6in (15cm) in diameter.

The African tiger lotus is actually a form of water lily and it may produce its characteristic large white flowers, which will open at night, at the water's surface. Purchased in the form of a tuber, this lily is best planted in a container where it will soon start to grow readily. If it does flower, the seeds can be allowed to fall back into the water where they may grow if undisturbed. Vegetative propagation from the shoots is also possible.

As well as this red variety there is a green form; only one of these lilies should be housed in anything other than a large aquarium though, as their centrepiece effect will be otherwise lost. Fish often appreciate the cover provided by their large leaves.

Red ludwigia *Ludwigia repens*

LIGHT REQUIREMENT : bright

TEMPERATURE : 64–77°F (18–25°C)

SUBSTRATE : gravel

pH READING : neutral

WATER : soft–slightly hard

Members of this group of aquatic plants are found mainly in North America and dislike high water temperatures. Red ludwigia occurs naturally from the southern part of the United States into Central America and the Caribbean.

There are two well-recognized leaf types. In one variety the leaves can be rather pointed, whereas in the other case they are much more rounded in shape. The coloration can be equally variable. In spite of their name, these plants can sometimes be green, as well as red, in colour.

Plant red ludwigia in groups in gravel. Here the plant should soon establish itself and will start to grow strongly. If you wish to increase the number of plants, the simplest way is to cut some stems from the rear of the display where they are unlikely to be missed. Choose those with roots visible, cutting them so that the shoot has some roots attached. The cuttings can then be set elsewhere in the gravel. If these plants start to lose their lower leaves, it is often a sign of inadequate lighting.

Twisted vallisneria *Vallisneria tortifolia*

LIGHT REQUIREMENT : bright

TEMPERATURE : 27–79°F (15–26°C)

SUBSTRATE : gravel

pH READING : acid–neutral

WATER : slightly hard

The upright growth which characterizes vallisnerias is still apparent in this form with its twisted leaves. There is some dispute about the relationships of various vallisnerias. This particular type grows to a height of about 8in (20cm) whereas the Asiatic form, sometimes described as a separate species–*Vallisneria asiatica*–can reach double this size. The edges of the leaves may also be slightly serrated.

Twisted vallisneria is relatively undemanding about its growing conditions, certainly in terms of water chemistry, but it does require well-lit surroundings if it is to thrive. Space these plants accordingly so that light can penetrate down to the substrate, illuminating the whole plant rather than just the upper part of the leaves.

In a large aquarium the giant vallisneria may be a better option. It originates from parts of southeast Asia. The red variety makes an attractive contrast with the more usual green form and it can be grown successfully in aquaria over 18in (45cm) in depth.

In the aquarium, vallisnerias are usually grown from runners.

Wheat plant *Sagittaria graminea*

LIGHT REQUIREMENT : bright
TEMPERATURE : 64–79°F (18–26°C)
SUBSTRATE : gravel
pH READING : neutral
WATER : slightly hard

One of a number of related species which originate from the New World, the wheat plant itself grows from North America through to Mexico and parts of the Caribbean. There are several different varieties which typically vary in terms of the length, width and shape of their leaves.

Wheat plants grow well when permanently submerged in an aquarium, although in the wild they may spread as much above the surface of the water as below it. Out of the water, much broader elliptical leaves will be produced. The flowers are small.

Sold as runners, wheat plants can be cultivated quite easily as they are generally undemanding in their requirements. They will thrive even where the level of lighting is relatively low, but they will grow better in bright light.

Divide the runners into small groups, with some space between the individual plants so that the clumps can develop without becoming overcrowded. As with other similar aquatic plants, always set wheat plants so that their crowns are not buried in the substrate. Otherwise, they are likely to rot away rapidly rather than producing new growth.

Indian fern *Ceratopteris thalictroides*

LIGHT REQUIREMENT : bright
TEMPERATURE : 68–77°F (20–25°C)
SUBSTRATE : gravel and peat
pH READING : acid
WATER : soft

This aquatic plant, also sold as Sumatran fern, is found throughout tropical parts of the world and is versatile in its growing habits. When kept permanently submerged, its leaves are quite finely divided and a relatively pale shade of green; this is probably when it is at its most attractive. If allowed to float in the aquarium, the plant's coloration becomes darker with its whitish roots trailing down to provide cover and shade for those fish which usually frequent the top part of the aquarium.

Indian fern reproduces by means of small plantlets, which form on the edge of the leaves. These can be removed and planted elsewhere once they reach a diameter of about 1.5in (4cm). Good lighting is essential for Indian fern, or its leaves will die back. In good conditions, and in deep water, it can grow to nearly 24in (60cm) in height.

Water cabomba *Cabomba aquatica*

LIGHT REQUIREMENT : bright
TEMPERATURE : 59–79°F (15–26°C)
SUBSTRATE : gravel
pH READING : acid
WATER : slightly hard

These aquatic plants grow mainly in ditches and relatively calm areas of water from southern Mexico down to Brazil. In the aquarium therefore, it is best to keep them away from air stones and similar disturbances as this will have a detrimental effect on their growth.

Water cabomba can be grown very easily from cuttings weighed down into the substrate of the tank. Handle these stems carefully however, because they can be easily bruised and may then die off rather than root. It is a good idea to trim back the bottom two or three leaves and stick the stems into the gravel, allowing a little space between them.

Under good conditions, water cabomba cuttings can grow very fast, with pieces growing to 12in (30cm) or more in length. Trim back the shoots to maintain a fairly compact shape or long trailing lengths could effectively clog up the aquarium, detracting from its appearance.

Good lighting is essential when cultivating this plant or it will soon grow to the surface, losing its attractive feathery shape, while the lower leaves will go yellow and die back. On occasions, water cabomba may flower in the aquarium, producing relatively small flowers above the surface of the water.

Green cabomba *Cabomba caroliniana*

LIGHT REQUIREMENT : bright
TEMPERATURE : 59–79°F (15–26°C)
SUBSTRATE : gravel
pH READING : acid
WATER : soft

Occurring naturally in an area from south-eastern USA through Central America as far south as Argentina in South America, these aquatic plants grow in slow flowing stretches of water. Accordingly, they should be kept away from currents in the aquarium. Green cabomba is actually dark green in colour; there is also a reddish form, confined to South America, known as *C. piauhyensis*, which is sometimes grown in aquarium surroundings as well.

Both types can be cultivated very easily from cuttings weighed down into the substrate of the tank. They should soon become established here and grow rapidly. Green cabomba is somewhat easier to grow than the water

cabomba as it is less fastidious about growing conditions, often requiring less light.

On occasions, green cabomba may flower in the aquarium to produce relatively small flowers which are either white or pink in colour. Conversely, poor growth may indicate unsuitable water conditions–this plant will not thrive in alkaline water.

Red cabomba *Cabomba piauhyensis*

LIGHT REQUIREMENT : bright
TEMPERATURE : 59–79°F (15–26°C)
SUBSTRATE : gravel
pH READING : acid
WATER : soft

The red cabomba is found in Central and South America. The distinctive feature of this plant is the arrangement of its leaves, which are aligned on the same level rather than above each other as in the case of other cabombas. The coloration of the red cabomba is also different, with both leaves and stems having a reddish suffusion.

The growth of this cabomba tends to be less bushy than related species and it should be planted in well-spaced clumps as it has a high light requirement. If it yellows, this is often a sign of an iron deficiency, which can be overcome with an aquarium plant fertilizer, rather than inadequate lighting.

Madagascar laceplant

Aponogeton madagascariensis

LIGHT REQUIREMENT : medium
TEMPERATURE : 59–77°F (15–25°C)
SUBSTRATE : water
pH READING : slightly acid
WATER : soft

This unusual aquarium plant will not root if simply put into the substrate. It grows from a rhizome or tuber and is so called because of the strange, lace-like structure of its leaves. Although the leaves may appear to be weak they are actually surprisingly strong, with the spaces in the leaf structure serving to lessen water resistance. Beware of growing Madagascar laceplants in an aquarium where there is heavy contamination with algal growth however, as this will spread to the leaves and cause them to rot.

Madagascar laceplants are not easy to cultivate in the aquarium in any event. The tubers will grow well initially but they often start to die back and ultimately rot away. When starting out with them choose only good sized tubers, which can be up to 4in (10cm) long, and divide them up. These plants do sometimes produce flowers, which are white at first and then, after being

fertilized, they turn pink. Unfortunately, it has also proved very difficult to grow seedlings successfully.

Dwarf hygrophila *Hygrophila polysperma*

LIGHT REQUIREMENT : bright
TEMPERATURE : 59–86°F (15–30°C)
TANK DISTRIBUTION : background
SUBSTRATE : gravel
pH READING : acid
WATER : soft–hard

Originating from south-eastern Asia, the dwarf hygrophila is a very easy aquatic plant to culti-vate in aquarium surroundings, provided that there is not a large population of snails; they are likely to strip the leaves of this plant in preference to almost all others growing in the tank.

Cuttings need to be weighed down in groups, and they should soon root and grow to form a dense clump of plants. They can also be arranged in a line to provide good cover at the back of the aquarium. Although very undemanding in terms of its own growing requirements, dwarf hygrophila will tend to make the aquarium water more acidic.

Further pieces of the plant can be broken off and used as cuttings, with the thin stems becoming quite woody once the plants are established. The growth of dwarf hygrophila is such that it will spread rapidly, and you may need to curtail its growth. Pruning may be beneficial for older plants.

FLOATING PLANTS

Water lettuce *Pistia stratiotes*

LIGHT REQUIREMENT : bright
TEMPERATURE : 68–86°F (20–30°C)
SUBSTRATE : water
pH READING : neutral
WATER : soft

These floating plants can be very valuable in the aquarium, offering cover for the fish and screening part of the water surface, which creates suitably darkened areas for catfish and others which tend to avoid bright light.

Water lettuce itself will not thrive without good artificial lighting in the aquarium, but it must not come into contact with the droplets of condensation on the cover glass–if allowed to drip down persistently on to the plants, the droplets will cause the plants to turn black and die off.

Under favourable conditions however, water lettuce will grow very rapidly with small plants developing as offshoots on stolons connected to the adult plant. These stems rot away in due course, leaving the young plants on their own. As they grow, their white roots will turn black–this is quite normal and not a sign of fungal attack. Water lettuce can grow to a good size in suitable surroundings, with its leaves reaching a length of 10in (25cm), but this is unlikely within the confines of the aquarium.

Choosing and Introducing Fish

CHOOSING THE FISH

A wide range of fish is likely to be found in larger retail outlets. If there is a particular species which you are looking for however, you may need to find a specialist supplier either locally or via the columns of the fishkeeping magazines. The main advantage of purchasing stock locally is that the fish should already be fairly accustomed to the water conditions in your area.

It is often possible to gain an impression of the overall quality of the fish simply by the condition of the display tanks. If these appear clean and well labelled, then it is likely that the fish themselves will be in good condition. Beware of any in tanks where other individuals appear dead or ailing. A number of diseases are spread via the water and the stress of a subsequent move could trigger illness when you take apparently healthy fish home. If you are in any doubt, the safest recommendation is not to buy the fish.

Healthy fish will swim readily, although bottom dwellers such as some catfish may prefer to hide away. A danger sign is fish which appear to have difficulty in maintaining their position in the water, especially if their belly appears swollen, which indicates dropsy.

Any obvious damage to the fins can be a source of future worry, because fungal

A special aquarium net of suitable size is an essential piece of equipment for all fishkeepers, enabling most fish to be caught with minimum disturbance.

Try to encourage the fish into a clear stretch of water then bring the net up and under it from below, rather than from the side.

Azolla *Azolla filiculoides*

LIGHT REQUIREMENT : bright

TEMPERATURE : 68–79°F (20–26°C)

SUBSTRATE : water

pH READING : acid–neutral

WATER : slightly hard

This aquatic ornamental fern originates from the Americas and is widely grown in aquaria, where it provides valuable cover. The hairy leaves often overlap each other, creating a structured pattern. Good lighting is essential for azolla; under suitable conditions, it reproduces very rapidly by means of spores. Each leaf consists of two lobes, within which is a blue alga found nowhere else in the world. This alga binds atmospheric nitrogen, with the result that these plants are used as fertilizer in some parts of Asia.

Azolla is not necessarily a good plant to choose if you are feeding mosquito larvae to the fish however, as it has actually been used as a biological means of controlling these insects. The larvae are unable to reach the surface with their breathing tubes through the azolla and so die before they can complete their life cycle.

Choosing a healthy fish

1 The fish should not be gasping

2 Check that the eyes are not cloudy or swollen

3 Gill covers should be close to the body

4 Look for ulcers or other skin damage

5 Ensure that there are no abnormal swellings on the body

6 The fish should appear well muscled

7 No droppings should trail from the vent

8 Fish should be swimming without difficulty

9 Fins should not be ragged or damaged

10 Check that body coloration is normal

11 Fish should not have white spots

infections could develop on this part of the body. Provided water conditions are good however, and you can isolate the fish, the fins should grow back normally in due course. Those species with elaborate finnage, such as angelfish, are most at risk.

Look closely among the fish for any signs of the parasitic ailment known as white spot. While it is possible to curb the effects of this illness it can be very debilitating and spreads easily through the water.

The colours of fish can differ, both between individuals and also due to other factors, such as the lighting conditions. The fact that a fish may look paler than some of those shown in this book is not necessarily an indicator that it is ill.

Fish are usually caught by means of an aquarium net and then transferred to a large plastic bag which is just partially filled with water. Oxygen is forced into the bag to ensure that the fish have sufficient to last them for the journey home. Take them home straightaway, keeping the bag shaded from sunlight.

INTRODUCING THE FISH

Fish can generally survive a gradual fall-off in temperature, but this can be stressful. On arrival, do not simply tip them straight into the waiting, warm aquarium and subject them to further stress. Instead, allow the water in which they are being kept to warm up again by floating the bag on the surface of the aquarium for 30 minutes or so.

When you are ready to transfer the fish use a net to catch them. It is a good idea to avoid adding any of the water from the bag, because this will be more contaminated than the tank with bacteria, fungi and other potentially harmful microbes.

The fish will probably hide at first. Keep the aquarium lights off at this stage to allow them to settle. There will be little point in feeding them for a day or so because they are unlikely to eat initially.

The Nitrogen Cycle

1 Beneficial bacteria are vital to the wellbeing of the fish, especially in the aquarium
2 Fish produce waste from food
3 Waste is broken down by bacteria through a series of chemical reactions
4 Oxygen is needed for the functioning of the aerobic bacteria in the filter bed
5 Bacteria convert toxic ammonia to much safer nitrate, a plant fertilizer
6 Fish may eat the plant as food

The use of a water conditioner will help the fish to settle in their new quarters, as it removes the potentially toxic effects of chlorine compounds from tap water, and may protect their bodies from infection. There is normally a protective layer of mucus covering the body and if this is breached the fish is at greater risk of developing ulcers or fungus. If you ever have to handle a fish directly therefore, be certain that your hands are wet beforehand as you are then less likely to injure it.

It is also useful to add a filter conditioner to the water. Under normal circumstances, beneficial bacteria break down the ammonia excreted by the fish to nitrite and then to relatively harmless nitrate. The nitrate is then used by plants in the aquarium as a fertilizer. At first however, in a new set-up, the beneficial bacteria are not properly established and there is likely to be a build-up of ammonia which will be harmful to the fish. This build-up is sometimes described as the 'New Tank Syndrome', and problems are most likely to occur during the first six weeks.

It is therefore often recommended not to stock the aquarium to full capacity from the outset because this will exacerbate the situation. Instead, add quite hardy fish such as various barbs at first, followed by more delicate species such as tetras, for example, which prefer 'older' water. It will however be advisable to quarantine new arrivals for a fortnight in separate quarters; you can then be certain that the new fish are healthy and feeding properly before adding them to an established community aquarium.

Floating the bag containing the fish on the surface of the aquarium when you get home will minimize stress as it raises the temperature of the water within.

When you cut the bag, with a pair of scissors, avoid tipping the water from the bag into the tank-catch the fish instead.

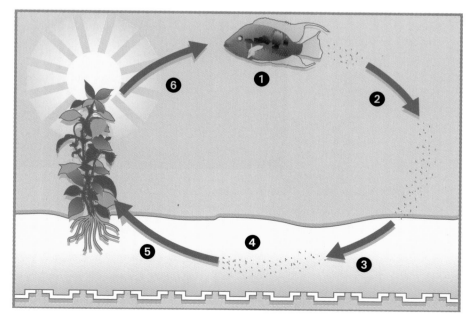

Feeding

FORMULATED FOODS

While some fish are essentially carnivorous, others feed primarily on vegetable matter–but it is not just the fish's diet which is significant in terms of the food that should be offered to them. The level in the aquarium which the fish inhabit is also an important consideration. While flake food which floats at the surface is readily eaten by many fish others, such as a number of catfish, will seek their food on the floor of the aquarium and so should be offered special pellets which will sink there rapidly. Floating foodsticks or pellets are an ideal option for larger fish which prefer to take their food at the water's surface, and there are also colour-enhancing foods available.

Such formulated foods are widely available and have meant that it is possible to feed aquarium fish simply and safely. Formulated foods need no special storage conditions, although they must be kept dry and used before the stated date on the packaging if the fish are to benefit from the vitamin content of the food.

LIVEFOODS

In contrast, livefood of various types will need to be purchased fresh on a regular basis, or you will have to establish cultures. While it may seem a good idea to offer fish natural foods such as tubifex worms, there is a very real risk of disease being introduced into the aquarium as a result. These particular worms are often found near sewage outlets.

River shrimps are often eaten by larger predatory fish, but they will not thrive in fresh water. These shrimps need to be housed in brackish water if they are to be kept for any length of time.

The safest of the aquatic livefoods are those which can be cultured by leaving a bowl of water outside. This is likely to attract mosquitoes which will lay their eggs there. The resulting larvae can be sieved out with a suitable tea-strainer and used as fish food, at least through the warmer months of the year in temperate regions of the world. Over time, if you have a large aquarium outdoors, you may be able to culture *Daphnia*–these are an excellent food for fish and promote good colouring, especially shades of red.

Concern over the safety of fresh livefood has prompted manufacturers to develop ways of treating them to avoid any risk. Freeze-drying has led to foods which can be stored in the same way as regular fish foods, although their dry nature means these tend to float at first making them less suitable for bottom-dwelling fish. This is not a problem with irradiated foods of this type, which need to be kept frozen; they come in small packets which must then be thawed out before being offered in small quantities to the fish. A wide range of animal foods are available in this form, including *Daphnia*.

The third option is to use terrestrial invertebrates which can be cultured quite easily in some cases at home. Whiteworm (*Enchytraeus*) is a typical example, with a clean, disused margarine tub and ventilated lid being required for this purpose. The tub should be partially filled with damp peat in which small pieces of moistened bread are buried, along with the starter culture of worms divided into groups. Kept warm and moist, the culture should be large enough to use in about a month or so. You can use tweezers to pull out the worms and separate them quite easily from the peat by washing them in a shallow pot of water from the aquarium before feeding them to the fish.

Wingless fruit flies (*Drosophila*) are another possible option especially favoured by surface-feeding fish such as hatchetfish (see page 52). A sealed yet ventilated tub containing banana skins should be adequate to encourage these flies to breed, although again the culture needs to be kept relatively warm. A number of these flies can then be tipped on to the surface of the water for the fish when required.

Always take care not to overfeed the fish. Err on the side of caution and only provide sufficient to be eaten within five minutes. Any uneaten food will simply pollute the tank. Several smaller snacks each day are therefore infinitely preferable to one large meal for the fish. It is important to check, particularly in a community aquarium, that the slower and sometimes shyer species are receiving sufficient to eat and you may need to use different types of food such as flake and pellets. You can also offer other items to provide variety. Vegetarian species may eat skinned garden peas, for example, but be prepared to remove anything left over after the fish have eaten.

dry flakes

cichlid pellets

vitamin-enriched tablet food

vegetarian food sticks

freeze-dried tubifex

freeze-dried blood worm

freeze-dried river shrimp

proprietary fry food

fresh blood worms

A range of the commercially available fish foods. You can also use other less traditional items such as small pieces of lettuce.

Breeding

Aside from looking at the fish in the aquarium, one of the most fascinating aspects of their care is breeding them. Almost all but the very largest fish covered in this book have been bred successfully, although some represent a much greater challenge than others in this regard.

PREPARING FOR BREEDING

You will probably need to invest in further tanks if breeding is to result in the rearing of young fish. Many species are bad parents in that they will eat both their spawn and fry if allowed to remain in the same tank, although some fish do show considerable devotion to their offspring. The mouth-brooding cichlids, for example, actually carry their eggs in their mouth until hatching occurs and then will often guard their fry for a period afterwards.

The first aim for successful breeding is to obtain at least one pair of the species concerned. Means of differentiating between the sexes are explained in the individual entries later in the book, although in some cases it may be better to have either a single male and several females, or vice versa.

A number of factors may influence spawning activity, but increasing the level of livefood in the diet is likely to be a significant factor. Changes in the water level or more frequent water changes, mimicking the effects of flooding in the wild, can also trigger breeding activity. Lowering the

water temperature slightly will also serve to duplicate the effects of a large influx of fresh water into rivers and streams following heavy rain.

As the time for spawning approaches male fish tend to become more colourful in many cases and females swell with eggs. The level of activity in the aquarium rises as the males pursue their intended mates. In some cases this can become quite vicious, to the point that the fish may have to be separated to prevent any fatalities. Take out the male and reintroduce him at a later stage once the female is likely to be closer to spawning.

Not all fish lay eggs. Some give birth to live offspring, and these fish have relatively few fry. This is partly due to the fact that the danger of losing them is reduced compared with the hundreds or thousands of eggs which are scattered at random by most egg layers. The majority of the eggs would fall victim to predators in the wild, with only a small proportion of the fry actually hatching. There is no placental attachment in the case of live-bearing fish however; the fry simply develop in fertilized eggs retained in the female's body and break free at birth. If you are interested in breeding livebearers, it is important to be aware that a single mating will enable a female to produce a number of broods in succession. The male in the tank may not, therefore, be the parent of the fry.

SETTING UP SPAWNING TANKS

The design of the spawning tank depends

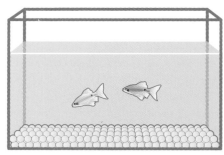

A spawning tank with marbles on the floor. This helps to prevent egg scatterers from consuming their eggs.

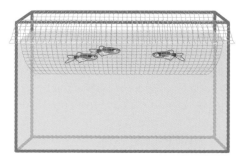

Another method is to confine the fish to the top of the tank so that their eggs will fall through the mesh to safety.

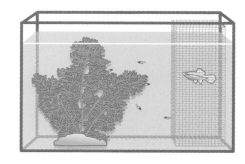

A tank for breeding livebearers. The female is confined in part of the tank until she has completed her brood. They escape out of reach.

One of the earliest indications of possible breeding could be increased disruption in the aquarium, with the dominant male fish driving away or even attacking potential rivals. Cichlids such as firemouths can become highly aggressive.

Spawning on rockwork. Most fish do not form a strong pair bond but if you are offered a proven pair, choose these rather than unproven stock. Not every breeding attempt ends in success and patience may be needed, especially at first.

on the species concerned but it is important to ensure that filtration is gentle. This applies especially in the case of the labyrinth fish, which construct bubble nests of saliva in which their eggs are deposited. Too much surface current at this stage will destroy the nest while later, once the fry have hatched, the aquarium must be kept covered because if they become chilled at the surface their labyrinth organs will be damaged.

You can obtain small heaters for spawning tanks. The smaller size can be helpful in deterring fish from laying their eggs on the heater, but it will be safer to place a mesh sieve around it. Avoid positioning the heater horizontally if possible, because once the fry hatch they may rest here and are liable to be fatally injured as a result.

REARING THE FRY

There is no set hatching period and much depends on the temperature of the water. When the fry do emerge from their eggs they will not be able to swim freely at first; instead, they rest and absorb the yolk sac which attaches to the underside of their body. Once the fry are swimming freely around the tank, they must be fed.

Commercial fry foods have simplified the rearing process for many smaller fry, although it is possible to set up cultures of infusoria quite easily. An outside tank that is partially filled with some hay or other vegetable matter should be sufficient. Very hot water should be poured into the container, which then needs to be left in a warm place. Watch the water as it turns

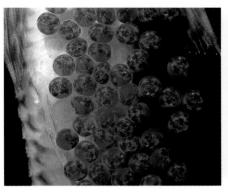

The breeding habits of egg laying fish in particular differ quite widely. While some may eat their eggs others will guard them until the fry hatch, which usually occurs within a few days.

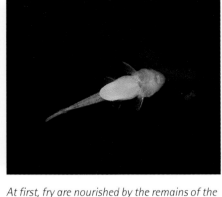

At first, fry are nourished by the remains of the egg sac after hatching. It can be seen here as the yellowish swelling on the underside of this young catfish.

cloudy and then clear, over a period of perhaps 5–7 days depending on the temperature. This is the stage at which infusoria will be present. Next, bale out portions of the water containing the microscopic infusorians and tip this into the rearing tank for the fry. Another possibility as an early food is cooked egg yolk, grated to a very fine consistency through muslin, though this is likely to pollute the water quite rapidly.

Young fish need access to an almost constant supply of food so that they can eat and grow quickly. However, the food that can be offered to the fry initially will depend upon their size. Cichlids, for example, are relatively large on hatching, whereas labyrinth fish are correspondingly much smaller.

One of the most widely used rearing foods for larger fry is brine shrimp *nauplii*, which are the larval form of *Artemia*. Their

eggs can be purchased from aquarist stores and hatched in accordance with the pack instructions without great difficulty.

Hatching will take at least 12 hours or so and sequential batches will be required to guarantee a supply of food for the young fry. Keep the brine shrimp *nauplii* eggs away from moisture by storing them in an airtight vessel, or their chances of hatching could be seriously reduced. *Nauplii* can also be introduced to the diet of smaller fry as they grow.

Since hundreds of fry may result from a single spawning, you will need to have additional tanks available so that you can separate the young fish into groups as they become larger. Otherwise, not only will their development be curtailed, but the risk of disease will be significantly increased by overcrowding. It is often possible to find aquatic shops or enthusiasts willing to take surplus stock.

Young discus will feed at first on special mucus which is produced on the sides of the bodies of their parents, nibbling here when they become free-swimming.

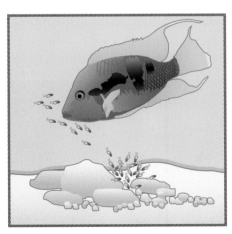

Some cichlids will spawn on the floor of their quarters, with the young also being guarded for a time in the spawning pit after hatching.

The mouth-brooding cichlids produce relatively few eggs, which are incubated in the mouth of the female. The young fry will dart back inside away from danger.

Health Care

MONITORING WATER CONDITIONS

If the water conditions are suitable for the fish, outbreaks of disease in the aquarium are unlikely. It is possible to check on the chemistry of the water by means of test kits or equipment such as a pH meter. These are easy to use and regular testing every week or so will warn you of any likely problems. Partial water changes need to be carried out to refresh the water in the aquarium, with perhaps 20% of the volume being siphoned out every 2-3 weeks. The discarded water should then be replaced by water of the same temperature which has been treated with a water conditioner.

Never be tempted to suck up aquarium water to start a flow of water through a piece of tubing, because bacteria and other harmful microbes are likely to be present in the water. Special siphons for aquarium use can be purchased from aquarist stores. In fact, a gravel cleaner siphon, which stirs up the gravel and removes solid particulate matter at the same time as the tank water, will help to lower the level of pollutants and will ensure that the under-gravel filter is functioning to optimum capacity. Take care, however, not to dislodge any of the aquarium decor or disturb the fish in this part of the aquarium when you are cleaning the gravel.

It is advisable to wear plastic gloves when dipping your hands into the aquarium because of the slight risk of piscine tuberculosis. This is not a serious disease in people, although it will result in an unpleasant skin condition which requires medical treatment.

A separate treatment tank is recommended, since medication may harm the beneficial bacteria in the main tank. Keep the decor simple, but provide some cover.

DIAGNOSING ILLNESS

It can be difficult to diagnose fish diseases in some cases without the help of a laboratory investigation and this is true with suspected piscine tuberculosis, although losses of fish in the aquarium will be high in this instance. Symptoms may include weight loss, bulging eyes (exophthalmia) and lethargy, but these can be associated with other diseases as well.

Not all apparent signs of illness may be the direct result of disease. If many of the fish show signs of discomfort, check the equipment; this applies particularly if the fish are gasping at the surface. An immediate water change may help to bring a rapid improvement in their condition while the actual cause can be further investigated and remedied.

Poisoning of the aquarium may also occur, so try to avoid using any sprays in the room where the aquarium is located. Treatments for other pets, such as flea sprays, are likely to be deadly for fish if the spray wafts on to the water. Fish suffering from poisoning often swim round in circles with their fins clamped up tightly.

FUNGUS

One of the most common diseases seen in aquarium fish is fungus. It is generally a reflection of poor conditions or damage to the body or fins, with debilitated fish being at greatest risk of succumbing to illness of this type. The fungal microbes are widely distributed in nature and will inevitably be present in the aquarium water. Affected fish lose their colour with the fungal growth, resembling cotton wool or whitish slime, spreading over their bodies.

Proprietary treatments are available from aquarist shops and must be used strictly in accordance with the instructions. The fish should be moved to a separate tank with a plain cartridge filter, because filtration over carbon inactivates some remedies. Fish eggs are also vulnerable to fungus in some cases, and it may even be necessary to add a chemical of this type to the spawning tank to protect them.

A swollen abdomen is characteristic of dropsy. This ailment may result from either infectious or non-infectious causes.

Fungus can strike anywhere on the body, especially where there is an injury. If detected at an early stage, treatment should be successful.

Damage to the scales can also result in bacterial infections, giving rise to ulcers. As well as treating the condition, check the water quality.

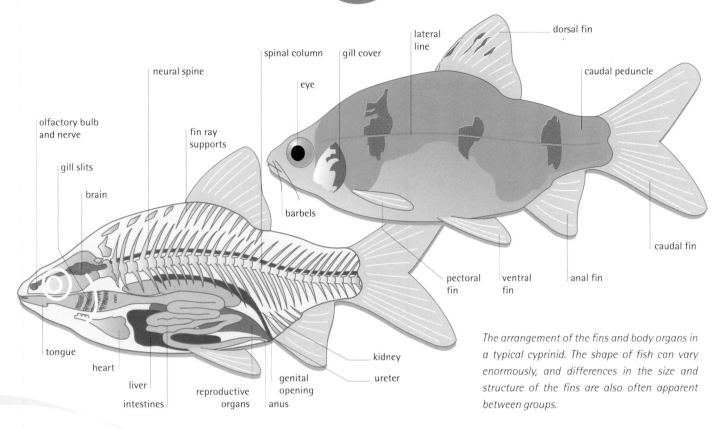

neural spine

olfactory bulb
and nerve

gill slits

brain

spinal column

eye

gill cover

lateral
line

dorsal fin

fin ray
supports

barbels

caudal peduncle

caudal fin

tongue

heart

liver

intestines

reproductive
organs

genital
opening

anus

kidney

ureter

pectoral
fin

ventral
fin

anal fin

The arrangement of the fins and body organs in a typical cyprinid. The shape of fish can vary enormously, and differences in the size and structure of the fins are also often apparent between groups.

WHITE SPOT

This remains a common disease and is caused by a unicellular protozoal parasite called *Ichthyophthirius multifiliis*; it is often known as 'Ick' or 'Ich' for this reason. An epidemic can develop in the aquarium from just one single affected individual. The white spots break down giving rise to tomites, which are the free-swimming stage in the life cycle. There can be as many as 1000 tomites from each spot and, within the confines of an aquarium, they will have no difficulty in finding other fish to infect. The tomites attack the skin, opening the way for other microbes such as fungi and bacteria to invade the body.

The white spots themselves are hard to destroy and so treatment is aimed at killing

the tomites. A range of remedies for this purpose are available from aquarist outlets. Keeping new fish isolated should ensure that the disease does not then spread into the main aquarium where treatment will be much harder. Always follow the instructions for using such remedies carefully. There will be no benefit in overdosing the sick fish; in fact, this could well prove to be harmful and may well result in its demise.

Other parasitic problems do crop up on occasions, but they are relatively rare compared with white spot. Gasping, for example, could well be indicative of gill flukes, concealed under the gill covers. Always suspect a parasitic problem if the fish is rubbing itself against decor in the aquarium, although there could be other causes for this behaviour–notably the fact that you may not have added the water conditioner when carrying out a water change, thus allowing toxic chlorine into the aquarium.

ANATOMY OF THE FISH

The shape of fish can differ quite widely; some have a broad shape, while others have narrow, cylindrical bodies. The typical outline of a fish is shown above. The fins are essential for swimming, helping the fish to control both the direction and speed of its movements. The gill covers, or opercula,

protect the sensitive gills which are hidden beneath. The gills themselves enable fish to extract oxygen from the water so they can effectively breathe underwater.

Fish rely heavily for sensory input on the lateral line which runs down each side of the body, although some groups do have good eyesight. This jelly-filled canal detects vibrations in the water, warning the fish of danger or obstructions in their path. Some fish have barbels around their mouths which have a sensory function, helping the fish to find their way around their environment and to locate food particles.

Fish are vertebrates and have an obvious skeleton. The shape of their body gives an indication of where in the water they will be found. Those with a straight back are likely to remain close to the surface. In contrast, fish with broad bodies will spend much time in the middle stretches of water where they will be able to swim without difficulty. Mouth shape provides further clues; those fish with upturned mouths are likely to be surface feeders, whereas many catfish, for example, with mouths situated low on the head, are likely to seek their food at the bottom of the tank. Buoyancy in the water is achieved by means of a swim bladder which is filled with air, although this structure is not present in all fish.

A fish showing the characteristic white spots on its body is a serious hazard to other fish in its aquarium.

CYPRINIDS

There are about 1500 different members in the family Cyprinidae, of which the goldfish (*Carassius auratus*) is the best known coldwater species. Cyprinids can be recognized by the absence of an adipose fin behind the main dorsal fin on the back. They also have sensory barbels around the mouth which help them to find food in murky waters. Barbs, rasboras and danios are the most widely kept cyprinids in tropical aquaria. They originate from parts of southern Asia and Africa.

It is worth bearing in mind that these fish will often damage aquarium plants, but offering green food as part of their regular diet may deter such behaviour. Their teeth are not in their mouth, but further back in the throat (pharyngeal) area. All cyprinids reproduce by laying eggs which are scattered at random around the aquarium during spawning. Many cyprinids are relatively social by nature and most can be kept in shoals without problems.

Rosy Barb *(Barbus conchonius)*

If you are setting up an aquarium for the first time, rosy barbs are a good choice as their care is straightforward and a pair may well spawn successfully. These attractive fishes originate from north-eastern India and they are commonly found in waterways in Assam and Bengal.

A tank for these barbs does not need to be very large, although it should be densely planted with subdued lighting above. Floating plants on the water's surface will serve to diffuse the light from above.

Sexing rosy barbs presents no problem since males can be distinguished by their predominantly pink fins, whereas those of females tend to be virtually colourless. Their body coloration becomes noticeably brighter as they come into breeding condition. At this stage, the male will pursue a female relentlessly until she spawns among the plants in the substrate.

The eggs must then be removed from the adult fish or they will eat them. It may be simpler to transfer a breeding pair to a relatively shallow spawning tank, which will allow the eggs to hatch where they were laid. The adult fish can be returned to their permanent quarters after spawning. The development of the eggs is rapid, with the young fry emerging about a day later. They are relatively easy to rear and can be provided with a suitable commercial fry food once they start swimming around the tank, within several days of hatching.

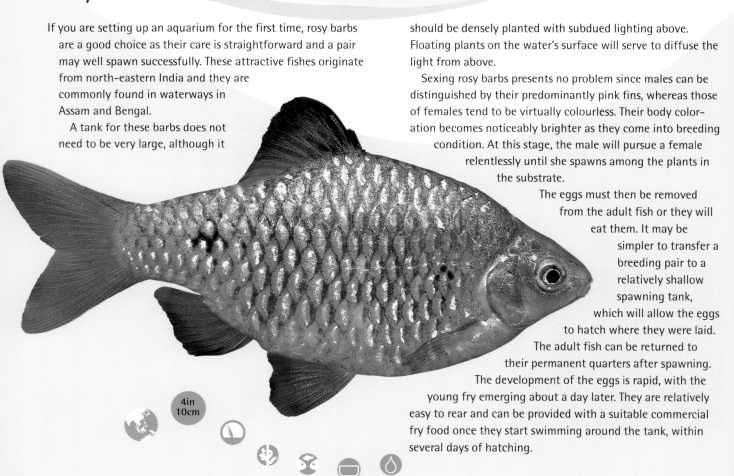

4in
10cm

Black Ruby Barb *(Barbus nigrofasciatus)*

Found in streams in the mountainous part of the island of Sri Lanka, these barbs agree well in groups. Male black ruby barbs have particularly deep bodies and, in spite of their small size, they are colourful fish, particularly as the time for spawning approaches. The rich red coloration on the head then assumes a purplish hue in males, which is why these fish are also known as purple-headed barbs. Their black markings become more pronounced at this stage too, resembling velvet in appearance.

Keeping two or more males together in the company of a group of females helps to maintain their coloration. Female black ruby barbs can be distinguished easily in any event since their dorsal fin is not solidly black, like that of the male, but is mainly transparent with the black area confined to the base.

Although active by nature, black ruby barbs will not be aggressive towards other tank occupants, making them a good choice for a community aquarium. A separate spawning tank is again recommended for breeding purposes. The eggs tend to be laid in the morning and hatching is likely to take place a day later. The fry start to swim about a week later although, as in other cases, this depends to some extent on the temperature of the water, which should approximate to that of the main aquarium.

3In
7.5cm

Tinfoil Barb *(Barbus schwanenfeldi)*

While the majority of *Barbus* species are relatively small, the tinfoil barb will rapidly outgrow a community aquarium–so bear this in mind before purchasing youngsters. However, they are very attractive fish, with shiny, silvery bodies reminiscent of tinfoil and a variable reddish shade to their fins set alongside black markings.

Tinfoil barbs will rapidly destroy most aquatic vegetation and are therefore best kept in an aquarium with plastic plants. As they grow larger, they prey on smaller fish. Large *Hypostomus* and similar catfish make ideal companions however, since their sluggish natures mean they will not come into conflict with these fairly boisterous barbs.

It is important that an aquarium housing tinfoil barbs is covered because they may otherwise leap out of the water, with catastrophic consequences. Breeding has been achieved where these fish can be kept in a group. There is no obvious visual means of distinguishing the sexes until the female is ready to spawn.

12in
30cm

Tiger Barb *(Barbus tetrazona)*

Tiger barbs are also sometimes called Sumatra barbs, although they do occur elsewhere in south-east Asia as well. They are probably the most widely kept of all barbs, and can be instantly recognized by the four black stripes crossing their body. Males are again more colourful than females, with reddish tips to their fins and a redder tone to their faces.

Tiger barbs can sometimes prove to be disruptive in a community aquarium, especially when housed with other fish which have elaborate fins, such as angelfish (*Pterophyllum* species). These barbs often display a tendency to nip at fins, damaging them as a result, so their companions need to be chosen with care. Well-oxygenated water is essential for tiger barbs; if the oxygen level is poor, the fish will cluster at the surface adopting an almost vertical posture.

Female tiger barbs may produce as many as 700 yellowish eggs at a single spawning. Rearing presents few problems, provided that the water quality is maintained. The fry are free-swimming about 5 days after hatching and can be fed satisfactorily on proprietary foods.

A number of colour variants of the tiger barb are also now established. These include an albino, where the dark markings are missing and the eyes are red, as well as a red-bellied form called the 'Hong Kong albino'. In some albinos, the gill covers may be missing–the breeding of such fish is not recommended. There is also a shiny moss-green form with a dark body, and a distinctive yellow variant.

3in
7.5cm

Two-spot Barb *(Barbus ticto)*

The two-spot barb originates from parts of India, ranging up into the Himalayas as well as occurring in Sri Lanka. It is not easy to distinguish the sexes outside the breeding period, although females typically lack any dark markings on their dorsal fin. These will be apparent in the case of the male, especially close to the edge of the fin. The spots which give these fish their name are present on the sides of the body.

Two-spot barbs were first kept in aquaria back in 1903. A variant of the species was documented in the Ukrainian city of Odessa in 1971, although its precise origins are unclear. It was first seen in Europe during the following year, and also attracted the attention of fishkeepers in Moscow. Now known as the Odessa barb, this fish may be a naturally occurring sub-species from a yet undiscovered locality.

Smaller than the two-spot barb, Odessa barbs are relatively slow to develop their red coloration, which may take 6–12 months to become apparent in males. Colour feeding and plenty of livefood will help to ensure its richness. Breeding in either case is relatively straightforward, with several males being housed in a suitable spawning tank in the company of a female for this purpose.

4in
10cm

Golden Dwarf Barb *(Barbus gelius)*

This fish is one of the smaller barbs. It occurs in parts of north-eastern India and its distribution extends to Bengal. The dark markings on its body distinguish it from the golden barb (*B. sachsi*), which is also significantly larger in size.

Sexing is quite difficult, but in males in good condition the dark gold stripe running down the sides of the body may assume a coppery hue in the vicinity of the caudal peduncle. Males are also likely to be less rotund in shape than females.

Golden dwarf barbs are active fish which show to good effect in shoals. Incorporating a relatively dark bottom to the aquarium can serve to highlight their coloration.

A special aquarium should be set up for egg laying. About 100 eggs will result from a single spawning; the adults should be removed afterwards because they consume their eggs, which adhere to suitable aquatic plants. The hatching and rearing of these fish does not differ significantly from that of other members of the genus. The fry hatch within a day or so and digest the remains of their yolk sac before they become free-swimming. They will then search for food; proprietary diets are suitable for rearing at first.

Five-banded Barb *(Barbus pentazona)*

Originating from relatively warm waters in the Malay Peninsula and neighbouring islands including Sumatra, these barbs often appear to be rather less active than other barbs. There are five blackish bands encircling their bodies and another which passes through the eyes, although these markings may well be more distinctive in some individuals than others. Males of this species display red markings on their fins and are usually more brightly coloured overall.

This particular species can prove to be slightly more demanding than related barbs in terms of general care and feeding habits. It is often recommended that these fish are kept at a slightly warmer temperature, up to 86°F (30°C), especially to stimulate breeding activity. Small livefood such as whiteworm (*Enchytraecus*) should also feature in their diet at this stage. Newly acquired five-banded barbs should be watched carefully to ensure that they are eating properly as they can sometimes be reluctant to sample flake foods, preferring livefoods.

Fry are not very difficult to rear, particularly as they grow quickly, but be sure to avoid overcrowding them because they are very susceptible to poor water quality. Divide the young barbs into smaller groups therefore, as they grow larger.

Ember Barb *(Barbus fasciatus)*

This species is also sometimes known as the fire-glow barb in another reference to the reddish coloration evident on the body of the male, which becomes especially prominent at the start of the spawning period. Female ember barbs are significantly duller in coloration, with virtually transparent fins, and their reddish coloration is confined to a small area of the gill covers. They are otherwise pale yellow, becoming silvery on the lower part of the body, with a series of four broad and incomplete black bands apparent in both sexes. A further dark area is evident at the base of the tail.

For breeding purposes, it is a good idea to keep these barbs in groups comprising one male and two or even three females, because males have a reputation for being aggressive at spawning time. Use large marbles to line the floor of the tank because the eggs are highly adhesive and will stick to a spawning grid, where they are more likely to be eaten. Soft water is recommended for the rearing of fry; as they grow older they can be kept in harder water, provided that this transition is made gradually.

5in
12.5cm

Checkered Barb *(Barbus oligolepis)*

Originating from Sumatra and neighbouring Indonesian islands, this species is sometimes known as the island barb. The coloration on each of the scales of these barbs is responsible for their checkered appearance. The black markings here extend from the front to highlight the side of the scales as well. The fins of male checkered barbs have a decidedly reddish hue, with the dorsal especially being prominently edged with black. Their underparts may also be more colourful than those of females, especially as the time for spawning approaches.

Try to incorporate a relatively fine substrate on the floor of the aquarium–if this will not block the under-gravel filter–because checkered barbs like to excavate the floor of their aquarium, searching for morsels of food. Feeding is straightforward, as they will eat both flake food and livefood readily.

A spawning tank for checkered barbs should be planted with *Myriophyllum*, which will serve to catch the eggs and, hopefully, will be

dense enough to protect most of the spawn from the adult fish until they can be transferred back to their aquarium. Females which are ready to spawn become swollen in appearance and this in turn tends to highlight their markings.

These barbs can be kept safely in groups because although males may challenge each other, this is unlikely to develop into serious fighting. Young checkered barbs grow quickly under good conditions, and will themselves attain maturity from the age of four months onwards.

5in
12.5cm

Zebra Barb *(Barbus eugrammus)*

This species can be distinguished by the six dark stripes running along the sides of its body; it is sometimes called the striped barb. The zebra barb is referred to in older works under the scientific name of *Barbus fasciatus*; it closely resembles another barb which shares its common name but is identified scientifically as *Barbus lineatus*. However, the latter fish lacks the barbels around its mouth and is not presently being bred commercially.

The stripes of female zebra barbs are generally less distinctive, and may be less numerous, than those of males. The body shape of the female tends to be more rounded too, with a higher dorsal fin.

Zebra barbs are not aggressive towards smaller fish, although they do have rather nervous natures and are best kept in a well-planted aquarium.

Livefood, such as whiteworm, will serve as a spawning conditioner. A heavily planted aquarium is also recommended as a spawning tank, with the adult fish being removed as soon as possible afterwards, to safeguard the eggs.

Black-spot Barb *(Barbus filamentosus)*

The appearance of this barb changes quite noticeably as it matures. Young fish have a series of dark vertical bars running down the sides of their body, which become reduced to a dark area above the anal fin as they grow older. Their body coloration alters as well, from being a pale golden brown to a silvery shade of greenish–yellow.

Mature males can be easily recognized by the growth of trailing filaments on the top of their dorsal fins, which have a reddish appearance. Although the black-spot or filament barb can sometimes be confused in terms of its appearance with another species, *Barbus mahecola*, it has no barbels around the mouth.

Originating from mountain streams in southern India and Sri Lanka, black-spot barbs are particularly hardy, living without apparent discomfort at water temperatures down to 68°F (20°C). They do prefer a fairly open area for swimming at the front of the aquarium however, rather than a densely planted enclosure. As the time for spawning approaches, males develop whitish swellings on the upper lip and gill plates; this is quite normal and does not indicate ill health.

Arulius Barb *(Barbus arulius)*

This relatively large barb nevertheless makes a suitable occupant of a community aquarium, thriving when kept in small groups. Sexing is quite straightforward, with the dorsal fin being larger in the case of males. The female arulius barb has a less pointed tip to the fin. The dark markings apparent on the bodies of both sexes have an iridescent shimmer under suitable lighting conditions, with mature specimens tending to be most colourful.

Originating from southern parts of India, arulius barbs are quite active by nature and therefore need adequate space for swimming as well as a planted area where they can hide away. Feeding presents no difficulties, with a range of prepared foods such as flake food and other items, including small live-food, greenstuff like spinach and even algae being eaten readily.

Spawning may prove to be more problematical than with other species, particularly since these barbs produce relatively few eggs. Accommodating them in a spawning tank which is densely planted with fine-leaved plants such as *Myriophyllum* and *Cabomba* is generally recommended. Spawning occurs close to the water's surface and the plants will serve to protect the eggs, which typically number less than 100, until the adult fish can be removed from the tank.

4in
10cm

Cherry Barb *(Barbus titteya)*

These attractive little barbs were first kept by aquarists during the 1930s and, since then, they have become very popular. They can be sexed easily, as females are brownish with red fins while males display the characteristic cherry-red appearance. Their coloration becomes especially intense at the onset of the spawning period.

Unfortunately, they can also become more aggressive at this stage, pursuing females relentlessly, so that spawning tanks must be very well planted to provide adequate refuge for the female. The eggs, numbering up to 300, are laid in small clumps which attach to the plants. Feeding the fish with whiteworm during the spawning period should help to deflect their interest from eating their eggs as they are laid, but take care not to pollute the water with wasted food.

2in
5cm

Although cherry barbs can usually be persuaded to spawn without too much difficulty, rearing their correspondingly small fry can be quite difficult. Greatest success can be anticipated if rotifers are supplied as the initial fry food.

Being found in shaded waterways in their native Sri Lanka, these barbs require subdued aquarium illumination, with floating plants helping to diffuse the light. Although they are content in a community set-up, cherry barbs are solitary by nature.

Zebra Danio *(Brachydanio rerio)*

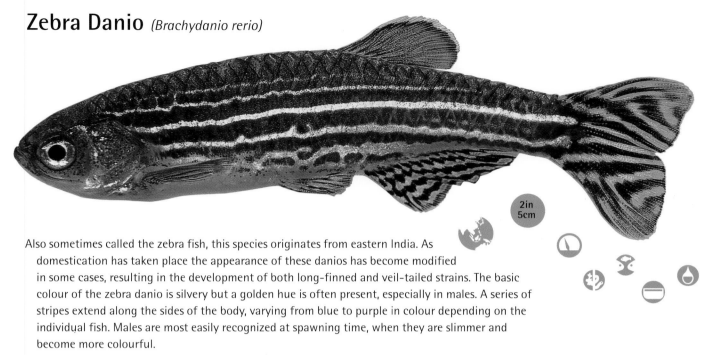

Also sometimes called the zebra fish, this species originates from eastern India. As domestication has taken place the appearance of these danios has become modified in some cases, resulting in the development of both long-finned and veil-tailed strains. The basic colour of the zebra danio is silvery but a golden hue is often present, especially in males. A series of stripes extend along the sides of the body, varying from blue to purple in colour depending on the individual fish. Males are most easily recognized at spawning time, when they are slimmer and become more colourful.

Zebra danios are very attractive fish that show well in shoals. They are unusual in forming strong pair bonds, even when kept in this way. Breeding itself is reasonably straightforward, provided that the adult fish cannot devour their spawn. A relatively shallow breeding tank, perhaps 6in (15cm) deep, will be required, with a grid on the floor serving to protect eggs which are dislodged from the plants there. Allow the female to become established in the tank and then transfer the male across as well. Keep the water temperature in the spawning tank slightly lower than in the main aquarium.

Spawning usually takes place in the morning, especially if the tank can be positioned so that gentle rays of sunlight fall on the water (without raising the temperature). Up to 400 eggs may be produced and these will start to hatch after about 2 days. About a week after egg laying occurs, the fry should be swimming around the tank. They can be reared on small livefoods such as brine shrimp *nauplii*.

Pearl Danio *(Brachydanio albolineatus)*

The coloration of these particular fish often appears to be highly variable, depending in part on the lighting conditions. The sheen on their bodies can be violet, especially towards the tail and over the gill covers. The fins are relatively clear, but they may show traces of red shading.

There is also a well-established yellow variant, with a golden body colour which is especially pronounced on the upper parts and the fins; it is sometimes called the yellow danio. Males in either case tend to be more brightly coloured than females, as well as being slightly smaller in terms of their overall size.

Inhabiting areas of fast flowing water in south-east Asia, extending to the island of Sumatra, pearl danios are powerful swimmers and should be housed in a reasonably long tank in spite of their small size. Feeding presents no problems with flake food being readily eaten, although the addition of small

livefood such as whiteworm to their diet is likely to stimulate breeding activity.

Their spawning tank should be planted with fine-leaved vegetation and, like the main aquarium, it must be covered to prevent the fish jumping out. Their breeding behaviour and requirements are similar to that of the previous species.

Leopard Danio *(Brachydanio frankei)*

These attractive danios are so
called because of their
golden coloration and dark
markings, which resemble
those of a leopard. In some cases
these spots are partially fused, creating
the impression of dark lines, especially close to
the tail. Their patterning extends down on to the
anal fin, and also over part of the caudal fin.

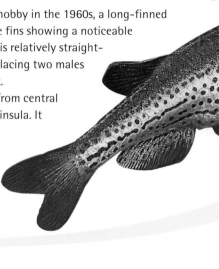

2in
5cm

   Since this species was introduced into the aquarium hobby in the 1960s, a long-finned
form of the leopard danio has been created, with all the fins showing a noticeable
increase in size compared with the wild form. Breeding is relatively straightforward, and fertility of the eggs may be improved by placing two males
in the company of a single female in the spawning tank.

   The natural distribution of the leopard danio ranges from central
and southern parts of India eastwards to the Malay Peninsula. It
has been suggested that it could actually be a naturally
occurring hybrid rather than a distinct species,
resulting from crosses between the zebra danio
(*B. rerio*) and the pearl danio (*B. albolineatus*).
Certainly, the leopard danio will hybridize readily
with both these species in aquarium surroundings.

Bengal Danio *(Danio devario)*

As its name suggests, the Bengal danio occurs in parts of northern
India and Bengal with a distribution extending eastwards to
Pakistan and Bangladesh. Males are usually slimmer and more
colourful than females, with a shallower body. This species can
be distinguished from all other danios by its longer dorsal fin.

   It is important to keep these fish in small shoals as single
individuals are likely to be nervous; this will be reflected in
their coloration, which will be paler than normal as a result.
Bengal danios grow quite large, but will be mature at about
half of their adult size. Their aquarium should be relatively
spacious and must include open areas for swimming, since
these fish are quite active by nature. Subsequent slow growth
of the young danios suggests poor water quality.

   As with other related species, these fish will feed mainly at
the water's surface and will take flake food
readily. Livefood should also feature in
their diet, particularly in the period
before breeding.

6in
15cm

   The fish should be removed
from their spawning tank once
egg laying has taken place. The
hatching period can last up to 2
days and the fry can normally be
reared quite easily. Subsequent slow
growth of the young danios is often
suggestive of poor water quality.

Giant Danio *(Danio aequipinnatus)*

As its name suggests, this is the largest of the danios; it used to be known under the scientific name of *Danio malabaricus*. The giant danio originates from south-western parts of India and Sri Lanka. It is pale blue in colour with three or four pale yellow stripes or blotches running down the sides of its body. The dominant individuals in a shoal tend to display the most vivid coloration.

Males have slimmer bodies than females, and their blue markings continue through to the tail fin in a straight line, whereas they tend to curve upwards in females. Giant danios are mature when they measure about 3in (7.5cm) long and they can usually be persuaded to spawn without too much difficulty.

Their breeding quarters should incorporate suitable plants or a spawning mop, as females scatter their eggs in batches through aquatic vegetation. As many as 300 may be laid in this way, with hatching then occurring within 2 days. When the female is ready to lay, shafts of morning sunlight falling on the tank will serve as a reproductive trigger.

The young danios must not be overcrowded while they are being reared, because this will have adverse effects on their growth rate. In spite of their size, these fish are not disruptive in an aquarium housing smaller species, although they will only attain their maximum size in a large tank.

Silver Shark *(Balantiocheilus melanopterus)*

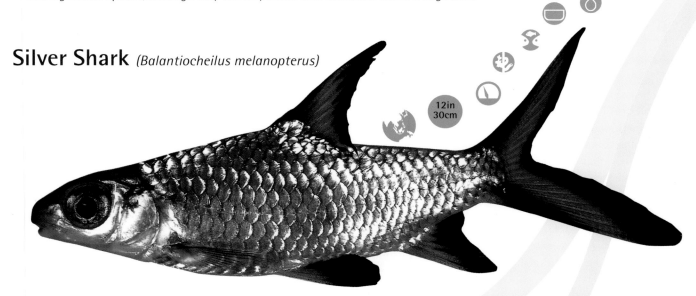

The sleek, slim profile, coupled with the tall, pointed dorsal fin and forked tail undoubtedly contributed to the common name of this fish, which is another member of the cyprinid family from south-east Asia. It is also known as the bala shark and the black edges to its fins are a characteristic feature. It is possible to sex large individuals, certainly once they reach a length of 6in (15cm); females have a more rounded underside to their bodies, especially between the pectoral and pelvic fins.

Silver sharks are active fish by nature and can jump, so care needs to be taken in catching them when the aquarium hood is removed. Although they feed readily on flake food, they will also consume plant matter and grub around in the substrate for particles of food there. Livefood such as tubifex is eaten readily.

Small individuals are not disruptive in a community aquarium, but it would be unwise to keep them with other fish which could be swallowed. Breeding details are essentially unknown at present, with spawning only likely to occur in a large aquarium. An odd characteristic of these silver sharks is the way in which they occasionally produce sudden sharp sounds. The reason for this is unknown.

Red-tailed Black Shark *(Labeo bicolor)*

Originating from Thailand, these cyprinids are unmistakable, having a velvet black body and a striking red tail fin. Red-tailed black sharks are not social by nature, although a single individual will agree well with un-related fish in a community aquarium. A densely planted environment with retreats where the fish can hide is recommended; submerged wood and rocks are ideal.

Although flake food will be eaten, the diet of the red-tailed black shark should include greenstuff such as lettuce. These fish will also consume algae growing in the aquarium.

Breeding is hard to accomplish in an aquarium, essentially because these fish have aggressive natures. A large set-up with the decor arranged so as to create natural divisions, enabling the fish to establish individual territories, offers the greatest likelihood of success. Females are capable of breeding at 3in (7.5cm) long, although it is virtually impossible to distinguish between the sexes with certainty outside the breeding season, at which stage the female swells with eggs.

Eggs will be deposited in a sheltered locality on the floor of the tank and will hatch within 2 days. Young red-tailed black sharks undergo a series of colour changes as they grow, starting off silvery-brown in appearance before becoming brown and finally black. The characteristic red tail only develops once the fish are about 7 weeks old.

6in
15cm

Red-finned Shark *(Labeo erythrurus)*

It is not difficult to tell this Thai species apart from the red-tailed black shark, since all its fins and not just its tail are reddish. There are other differences as well, with the body coloration of the red-finned shark being a greyish-green shade rather than black. An ornamental white variant is also commonly available now, lacking all trace of dark pigment. The body of these fish is therefore whitish, with orange markings evident on their gill covers and fins, and their eyes are distinctly reddish.

Red-finned sharks, also sometimes called ruby sharks, are far more amenable to the company of their own kind than their red-tailed relative, although they can be shy. Broken flowerpots set in the aquarium substrate are favoured retreats. Livefoods will again be eaten avidly by these fish and they will also graze on algae, with flake food providing the basis of their diet.

Males of this species are said to be recognizable by the black edge to their anal fin, while females swell with eggs as the time for spawning approaches. As many as 4000 eggs may be produced, with the fry being free-swimming by about 4 days old. They can be reared quite easily on brine shrimp *nauplii*, and require well-oxygenated, moving water.

6in
15cm

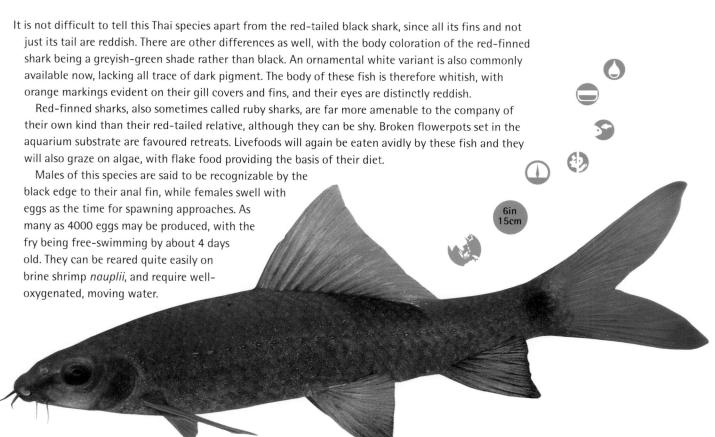

Flying Fox *(Epalzeorhynchus kallopterus)*

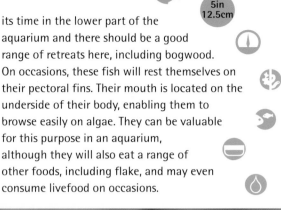

Ranging from northern India to south-east Asia, including islands such as Sumatra, the flying fox is a relatively amenable occupant of a community aquarium, although it can display territorial tendencies. It may ambush fish which approach too close to its domain, but it will not persecute these intruders by persistently chasing them around the tank. Its habit of swimming very fast on occasions can however cause a disturbance to other more placid aquarium occupants.

The flying fox has a streamlined, torpedo-like body shape and dark markings on its fins. The dark stripe running down the sides of its body continues on to its tail. It will spend much of its time in the lower part of the aquarium and there should be a good range of retreats here, including bogwood. On occasions, these fish will rest themselves on their pectoral fins. Their mouth is located on the underside of their body, enabling them to browse easily on algae. They can be valuable for this purpose in an aquarium, although they will also eat a range of other foods, including flake, and may even consume livefood on occasions.

Siamese Flying Fox *(Crossocheilus siamensis)*

Although similar in appearance to the flying fox, this species can be recognized without too much difficulty—firstly because its fins do not have the pronounced black markings, and secondly because it has just one pair of barbels, rather than two, on its upper lip. It is sometimes sold under the name of Siamese algae eater and since its introduction to the hobby in 1962, it has become very popular for this characteristic. Siamese flying foxes will not harm aquarium plants however, using their sharp jaws to rasp algae off surfaces instead.

These fish are found in flowing, well-oxygenated water, and they require similar conditions in the aquarium. They normally rest on or near the bottom of the tank and can use their mouths to anchor themselves on to a rock, for example, if faced with a strong current. Take care not to overcrowd Siamese flying foxes, as this will lead to displays of aggression. It is not possible to sex them by means of any external differences in appearance and, to date, their breeding details are essentially unknown.

Scissor-tailed Rasbora *(Rasbora trilineata)*

The scissor-like movements of the deeply forked caudal fin are responsible for the common name of this fish. The caudal fin may be decorated with yellow and blackish markings, while the other fins are transparent. The body colour is silvery-grey, with a black line extending down the abdomen to the tail and a gold streak above. A third dark line runs from the vicinity of the anal fin to the caudal fin, which explains why this fish is also known as the three-lined rasbora.

Unfortunately, sexing these rasboras outside the breeding period is difficult, although females may still have a more rounded appearance. However, since they show to best effect in small shoals, keeping them in a group should guarantee the presence of at least one pair.

Originating from parts of south-east Asia, scissor-tailed rasboras require a fairly secluded aquarium, especially for spawning purposes. The floor covering should be dark with dense planting around the sides and at the rear of the aquarium; in the case

of a spawning tank, the sides can be screened with dark paper.

The male will chase the female prior to egg laying, which usually occurs at night. Provided that the adult fish are well fed, they will not consume too many eggs before they are removed from the tank. The young hatch within a day, and can be reared in due course on brine shrimp *nauplii*.

3in
7.5cm

Pygmy Rasbora *(Rasbora maculata)*

This pretty fish shows to good effect in groups and is the smallest of all the cyprinids. It is also sometimes known as the spotted rasbora, because of the presence of three or more dark spots on its body behind the gill covers and adjoining both the anal and caudal fins. Males tend to be more brightly coloured than

females, especially at the onset of the spawning period; in addition, females typically have an extra dark spot above the anal fin on each side of the body.

Pygmy rasboras look very attractive as a group, kept with fish of a similarly non-aggressive temperament, or they can be kept in a large shoal in an aquarium on their own. Lighting can be used to enhance their red coloration. Feeding presents no difficulties and flake food will be taken readily, along with suitable small livefoods such as brine shrimp *nauplii*.

These rasboras rank among the easiest species to spawn, with only a small tank being required for this purpose. A suitable grid, to protect the spawn after egg laying occurs, is advisable, although feeding the fish well prior to transferring them here may help to deflect their attention away from the eggs. These are likely to be laid among vegetation and it is important to maximise the protection available for them, because pygmy rasboras produce only relatively small numbers–often no more than 50–at a single spawning. The resulting fry are correspondingly tiny, and need to be provided with rotifers as a first food if they are to be reared successfully.

1in
2.5cm

Pearly Rasbora *(Rasbora vaterifloris)*

The coloration of these fish, which originate from Sri
Lanka, can be quite variable. While some individuals
are basically pinkish in colour, others are decidedly
orange in appearance. As a result, they are sometimes
called fire rasboras. A bluish strain may also be seen on
occasions. Irrespective of their body coloration, pearly
rasboras all have obvious reddish suffusion on their
fins and males tend to be slightly larger than females.

Although social by nature, these rasboras have not
proved to be as hardy as some other members of their
genus and spawning may also be more difficult to
achieve. Pearly rasboras require a water temperature of
about 77°F (25°C) and water conditions are especially
significant for their successful maintenance and
breeding. Peat within the water or filter proves an easy
means of softening the water, making it more acceptable for these fish. A typical diet as offered to other
rasboras will suit them well; the occasional addition of
a colour food will improve their coloration.

A spawning tank for pearly rasboras should include
fine-leaved plants such as *Cabomba aquatica* or
Myriophyllum species, where the eggs will be
deposited. Hatching will occur about a day later, with the fry
becoming free-swimming in a further 4 days or so.

2in
5cm

Harlequin Rasbora *(Rasbora heteromorpha)*

The appearance of these rasboras, with a dark triangular patch
extending back from the abdomen to the base of the caudal
fin, is very distinctive. The silvery tone of the rest of the body
may be broken with yellow or reddish markings, which has
resulted in this species also becoming known as the red rasbora.
Males tend to be brighter in colour than females, with slimmer
bodies; females may be recognized by their more curved lower
profile, which gives them a broader body
shape when viewed from the side.

The espes rasbora (*R. espes*), which is sometimes considered to
be a subspecies of the harlequin rasbora, can be distinguished
easily by its orangish, rather than silvery, body and the black
mark behind the gill covers. It requires identical care, but has
gained a reputation for being harder to breed in aquarium
surroundings.

Harlequin rasboras are one of the most widely kept members
of this genus and will thrive in a relatively dark tank with
subdued lighting. Floating plants can be helpful in this case,
diffusing the light from above. Obtain a group of these rasboras
at the outset, as they have strong shoaling instincts.

A spawning tank for this species should include
broad-leaved plants such as cryptocorynes, since the female rasbora
will deposit her eggs in
clumps here after the
male has carried out an
elaborate courtship display.
Best breeding results are often
obtained with quite young females,
and as many as 100 eggs may be produced
in total. Soft water is essential for the successful
development of the fry, which are likely to start hatching
around a day later. They will be free-swimming after about
4 days and will require suitably small rearing food at first.

2in
5cm

Glowlight Rasbora *(Rasbora pauciperforata)*

This species is also called the red-striped rasbora because of the prominent red stripe which runs down each side of its body from the upper jaw to the base of the caudal fin. It has a very slender body shape and is an able swimmer, although rather nervous by nature. Females may again be recognized by their more curved ventral surface.

Glowlight rasboras require a similar tank set-up to related species, with a dark substrate being recommended. The aquarium should be densely planted at the back and around the sides, with a clear area at the front for swimming. The fish will dart back into the vegetation if disturbed.

Pairing these rasboras can be a problem, but allowing them to pick their own partners will give the greatest likelihood of spawning success. They show to best effect in shoals in any event, although they can be accommodated with other non-aggressive fish which require similar water conditions.

Small livefoods will serve as a good conditioner, although these are not the easiest of the rasboras to breed successfully. The spawn itself will often be deposited close to the roots of plants, and a peat base to the aquarium may be beneficial, as soft, acidic water will be essential in the spawning tank. Glowlight rasboras are not prolific, with females only producing perhaps 50–100 eggs at a single spawning. Remove the adult fish afterwards and the fry will start to hatch about a day later, although they are likely to be inconspicuous at first.

  2in 5cm

White Cloud Mountain Minnow *(Tanichthys albonubes)*

Discovered in the White Cloud Mountains near Canton in China, these fish live in clear, fast flowing mountain streams. They thrive at lower temperatures than most of the other fish in this book; keeping them in water heated above 77°F (25°C) may serve to shorten their life span. A thermostat setting of 64–72°F (18–22°C) is preferable for them.

White Cloud Mountain minnows live amicably in shoals, but new individuals added to an existing group will often spend more time on their own than in association with their companions. Water quality is very important, as these fish are naturally found in clean, well-oxygenated water. If conditions are less than ideal, they will be seen gulping at the surface and may have difficulty in swimming.

Sexing is reasonably straightforward, with females being distinguishable by their pale red lips and smaller size. White Cloud Mountain minnows are among the easiest egg layers to breed, partly because they will only rarely resort to eating the eggs after laying or to cannibalizing their fry. Therefore, it is not essential to set up a special tank for breeding purposes.

A slight increase in the water temperature should be adequate to ensure spawning. It is a good idea to provide fine-leaved plants, such as *Myriophyllum*, in the aquarium, where the female can scatter her eggs. Hatching usually occurs in about 2 days, and the young fish will be swimming freely within a week of hatching. A proprietary fry food can be used at first for rearing purposes.

The coloration of young White Cloud Mountain minnows is significantly brighter than that of adults and their iridescent blue-green will fade as they mature. These fish can breed from 6 months onwards and they may live for as long as 3 years.

2in
5cm

CHARACINS

The distribution of these fish lies primarily in the New World, although representatives of the group are also found in Africa. In total, about 1200 species are currently recognized and over 1000 of these are native to the Americas. The tetras are the most widely kept characins, but many other representatives of the group are also popular subjects for the tropical aquarium.

Characins can generally be identified by the presence of an adipose fin between the main dorsal fin on the back and the caudal or tail fin. They also have very sensitive hearing and this is due to the Weberian apparatus, which is a skeletal connection extending from the inner part of the ear to the swim bladder. Teeth are prominent in the jaws of many species, perhaps most notably in the case of the piranhas. Most characins will thrive in shoals, requiring well-oxygenated, clean water. Their feeding habits are varied, but the majority of those kept in aquaria show a preference for invertebrates of various types. Some, such as the notorious piranhas, are cannibalistic and are unsuitable for a community aquarium.

Glowlight Tetra *(Hemigrammus erythrozonus)*

Originating from the Essequibo River in Guyana, glowlight tetras were first kept in aquaria in 1933 and today they are bred commercially in large numbers for the aquarium trade. There is a distinctive reddish line which runs through the eye to the base of the tail and there is also a red area evident on the front of the dorsal fin.

In common with other tetras from this part of the world, the glowlight requires a well-planted aquarium with subdued lighting. Peat should be included in the system, to maintain the necessary water conditions; this is especially important when rearing fry, which can be susceptible to dropsy.

Female glowlight tetras have more rounded bodies than males, and tend to be slightly larger. However, accurate sexing is not necessarily vital at the time of purchase because you will probably have at least one pair within a group.

A separate tank is recommended for breeding purposes, as the eggs and any fry are otherwise likely to be eaten. Mature water, preferably from the established aquarium, will avoid too much of a shock to the adult fish when they are transferred.

Clumps of fine-leaved plants are important, but these should be spaced to allow the fish to swim among them. Fertility may otherwise be low, because of the way in which these fish mate. They roll over and touch fins on each occasion, with the female laying up to 200 eggs in batches in this fashion. These will tend to fall to the base of the aquarium, with the fry hatching about a day later. Aside from the typical form, there is now an established variety of the glowlight tetra which has a golden rather than red line extending down both sides of its body.

Buenos Aires Tetra *(Hemigrammus caudovittatus)*

As its name suggests, this particular tetra originates from the southern part of South America, occurring in the Rio de la Plata region bordered by Argentina, Paraguay and the south-eastern part of Brazil. Its coloration is more sub-dued than that of other tetras, being predominantly silvery with a pale bluish-green line running along its flanks. Orangish-red coloration is most marked on the lower abdomen, where it extends to the fins. Males tend to have redder fins than females and they may show a yellowish tone, becoming brighter in their overall coloration as the spawning period approaches.

Buenos Aires tetras are less demanding than some other tetras in terms of water conditions and can even survive in relatively cool water, down to 64°F (18°C). Feeding also presents no problems, with livefoods and formulated diets being eaten readily.

The only drawback of these fish is that they are likely to damage aquarium vegetation. It can be possible to deflect their attention from plants growing in the tank by providing small pieces of greenstuff such as lettuce on a regular basis, but if this fails plastic substitutes may be needed.

In addition, these tetras should not be kept with companions such as fighting fish (*Betta splendens*), which have trailing fins, as they can prove to be bad fin-nippers. Breeding is generally straightforward, although some females may prove to be aggressive towards potential mates. The eggs are deposited among plants and the fry can then be reared on brine shrimp *nauplii*.

3in
7.5cm

Beacon Tetra *(Hemigrammus ocellifer)*

The characteristic reddish spot above the eyes and the similar orangish area at the base of the tail underlie the common names of this fish, which also include the head-and-tail-light fish. It originates from the Amazon Basin, and makes an attractive addition to a community aquarium as it is easy to maintain on a diet of flake food and small livefoods, which help to stimulate spawning activity.

Breeding is reasonably easily accomplished, although recognizing pairs is not always straightforward. The most reliable means is the way in which a female swells with eggs. Males may have a white spot evident on close examination of the anal fin and this feature is especially evident at the onset of the breeding period.

The eggs will be scattered among fine-leaved plants in the spawning tank, usually quite early in the morning. As many as 300 eggs may be produced, with the fry hatching just over a day later. They need to be fed on a suitable fry food at first; by a week old, they should be able to eat brine shrimp *nauplii*.

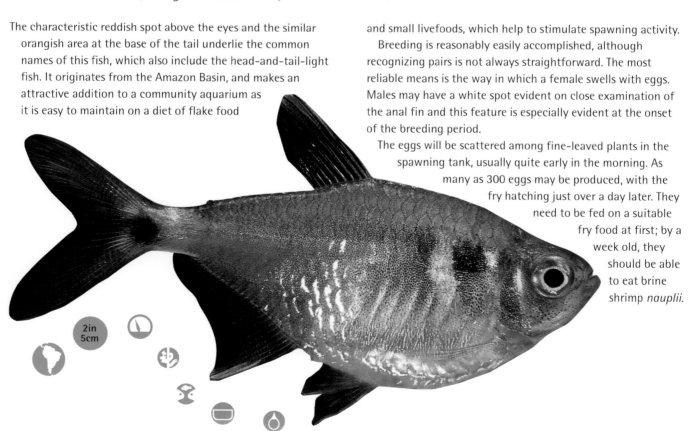

2in
5cm

Ahis Rummy-nose Tetra *(Hemigrammus rhodostomus)*

The unmistakable red area surrounding the jaws and extending back over the eyes is characteristic of these tetras, although in 1986 a slightly more colourful variant was named as the rummy-nose tetra (*H. bleheri*). There is also another rather similar species, called the false rummy-nose tetra (*Petitella georgiae*), in which the red area on the face divides into a stripe running down each side of the body. Black and white markings alternate across the caudal fin of adult fish in all three cases.

Both the *Hemigrammus* species will benefit from the addition of a black water extract to their aquarium, unlike the false rummy-nose tetra. Water quality is very important to the wellbeing of these fish, and they will not thrive in the presence of any significant concentration of nitrate–the recommended level must be below 30mg per litre.

2in
5cm

Although they will eat flake food readily a more varied diet, including small invertebrates, will be essential to trigger breeding activity. Females are most easily recognized at this stage by their broader profile. The spawning tank should be stood on a dark base and lined with dark glass marbles.

Rummy-nosed tetras will usually spawn on the base of the tank; they should be removed before they can eat their eggs. The fry will hatch about 36 hours after spawning and require a liquid fry food once they become free-swimming, around 4 days later. They can then be introduced to brine shrimp *nauplii* once they are about 10 days old.

Pretty Tetra *(Hemigrammus pulcher)*

This fish is also sometimes called the black wedge tetra, which is a reference to the darker area on the lower abdomen. It occurs in tributaries of the Amazon River in Peru, and was first introduced to the aquarium hobby in 1938. Its overall body coloration is silvery; darker colours and often a golden hue can also be apparent, depending on the lighting conditions and the age of the individual fish. A distinctive area of red coloration above the eyes serves as a further identifying feature. The body width is also greater in this species than in the case of other *Hemigrammus* tetras.

2in
5cm

Introducing these fish to a newly established aquarium, where the water is not yet mature, could give rise to difficulties. As long as water conditions are favourable, the care of pretty tetras presents no particular problems. Breeding is, however, more of a challenge with these tetras than most other species, largely because of compatibility problems. Starting out with a small group will again give the greatest likelihood of success.

The female can be recognized by her more rounded body shape. Wait until she is well rounded with eggs before transferring her to a densely planted spawning tank. If no eggs have been produced within 3 days, introducing a new potential partner is recommended. The eggs will be deposited among the plants, after which the adult pair should be returned to their aquarium. The fry can be reared in a similar way to other *Hemigrammus* species.

Black Widow Tetra *(Gymnocorymbus ternetzi)*

The coloration of these tetras alters significantly as they grow older. They are basically silver, with three dark bars running vertically down each side of the body that become darker towards the rear. The anal fin is a striking shade of velvety-black in young black widow tetras, but these dark markings change to a less attractive shade of grey as the fish matures, by about 12 months old.

Originating from parts of Paraguay, Bolivia and southern Brazil, this species was first introduced to fishkeepers in 1935; for many years, all the black widow tetras being kept were descendants of this original trio. As domestication has proceeded, a long-finned variety has developed which has now become well established.

The fins also provide a means of separating the sexes; the male's dorsal fin is more pointed than that of the female and the male's anal fin is broader at the front. Black widow tetras are one of the easiest members of this group to breed, also proving to be relatively hardy. Small livefood will serve as a good conditioner. Dense planting in the spawning tank is recommended, as it allows the fish to swim among the vegetation and deposit their eggs, after which they should be transferred back to the main aquarium.

Bleeding Heart Tetra *(Hyphessobrycon erythrostigma)*

Originating from the upper reaches of the Amazon in Peru, the bleeding heart tetra can be easily sexed since males have decidedly elongated dorsal and anal fins. The characteristic identifying feature of this fish is the reddish-pink heart-like marking on the sides of its body. The lesser bleeding heart tetra, another tetra with similar markings, but shorter, more rounded fins, was described from the Rio Negro during 1977, and this fish is known under the scientific name of *H. socolofi.*

These fish tend to rank among the more expensive tetras, because they are not easy to breed successfully. Newly acquired stock may also be relatively difficult to establish at first, being susceptible to fungus. Keeping them at a relatively high temperature around 82°F (28°C) can help the fish's own immune system to combat this type of infection.

For breeding purposes, small invertebrates such as wingless fruit flies can prove to be valuable conditioning foods. Keeping male and female fish apart during this period may also help to increase the likelihood of a successful spawning in due course. The water in the spawning tank itself should be soft.

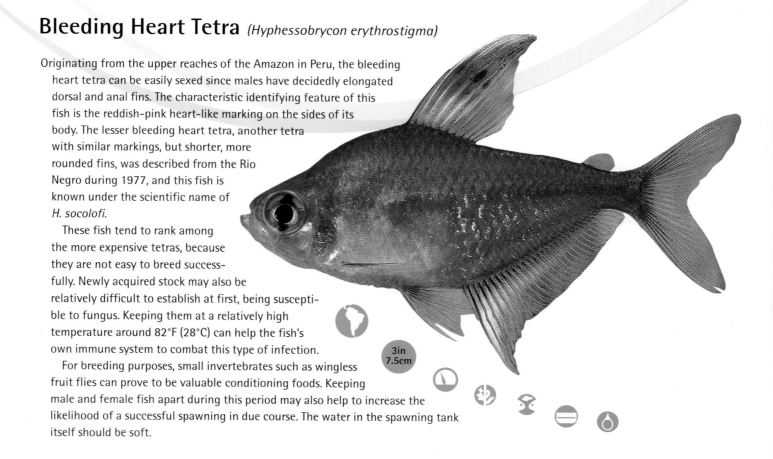

Lemon Tetra *(Hyphessobrycon pulchripinnis)*

Although lacking the bright coloration of some tetras this species can be an attractive addition to a community aquarium, especially when a small group of these fish are acquired. Mature males can be distinguished by the brighter yellow markings on their dorsal and anal fins, as well as being slimmer than females. Their coloration will deteriorate if the water is too hard. Feeding with a colour food can help to bring out their distinctive colours to best effect, particularly the red area around the eye.

2in
5cm

The lemon tetra is quite widely distributed through the Amazon Basin. It thrives under subdued lighting with open space for swimming, as well as a more densely planted area, in the aquarium. Spawning can be achieved successfully without too much difficulty, although a separate tank will again be necessary for this purpose. Increasing the water temperature slightly and offering livefoods can both serve as spawning stimuli.

The eggs themselves will be laid among fine-leaved plants, or even in the trailing roots of water hyacinth (*Eichhornia crassipes*), although any which descend to the floor of the tank are likely to be eaten, so a grid here may be helpful. Keep the spawning tank away from direct light, covering the sides with dark paper until the fry hatch. They can be reared quite easily, starting off with a diet of infusoria or a commercial substitute.

Yellow Tetra *(Hyphessobrycon bifasciatus)*

The coloration of these tetras varies between individuals. Some have a more yellowish suffusion, particularly along the back, than others which are therefore more silvery. This is a natural variation, with the more brightly coloured fish tending to be favoured by aquarists. Yellow tetras are quite hardy fish and they will thrive in a densely planted aquarium, preferably with reasonable movement of water. They originate from eastern parts of Brazil.

It is best to avoid housing them with fish with flowing fins, such as gouramis, because although they are not aggressive, these tetras may nip the fins of their companions on occasions.

Yellow tetras are one of the easier *Hyphessobrycon* species to spawn in aquarium surroundings. Males can be distinguished by the convex shape of their anal fins, whereas those of females are concave. In most cases, the male is also more colourful and slimmer in shape, especially as the time for spawning approaches.

It is better to condition the sexes apart, placing the female into the spawning tank first and then introducing the male subsequently. Spawning mops to provide dense cover are recommended, although fine-leaved plants can be used if preferred. Hatching and rearing requirements are the same as for other members of this genus.

2in
5cm

Black Neon Tetra *(Hyphessobrycon herbertaxelrodi)*

This particular fish is a different species from the
better known and more colourful neon tetra
(*Paracheirodon innesi*). It was discovered in a
tributary of the Rio Paraguay in the Mato Grosso
region of Brazil. The distinctive blackish area extends
for a distance below the iridescent greenish-blue
line on the fish's body, but does not colour the fins.
The upper part of the body is olive-green, while the
underparts are silvery. The coloration of the black
neon tetra can vary somewhat however, depending
on the water conditions and the lighting.

These tetras prefer rather dark surroundings
and show to best effect in small groups. They
have proved to be relatively easy to look
after and will breed well in aquaria. Livefood is
vital for conditioning purposes. As a general guide
females may be recognized by their deeper bodies
and more rotund appearance, especially as the time for
spawning approaches.

Hatching will occur after a period of about 36 hours and the young can be offered a suitable fry
food or infusoria at first, once they are free-swimming. Adult black neon tetras will benefit from a
good range of foods and will consume freeze-dried as well as live invertebrates of suitable size.

Rosy Tetra *(Hyphessobrycon rosaceus)*

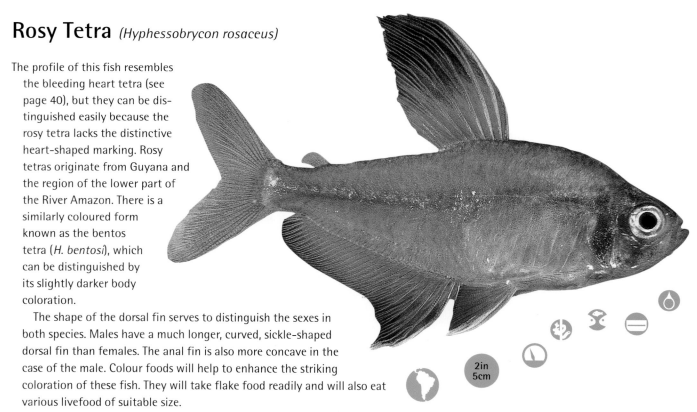

The profile of this fish resembles
the bleeding heart tetra (see
page 40), but they can be distinguished easily because the
rosy tetra lacks the distinctive
heart-shaped marking. Rosy
tetras originate from Guyana and
the region of the lower part of
the River Amazon. There is a
similarly coloured form
known as the bentos
tetra (*H. bentosi*), which
can be distinguished by
its slightly darker body
coloration.

The shape of the dorsal fin serves to distinguish the sexes in
both species. Males have a much longer, curved, sickle-shaped
dorsal fin than females. The anal fin is also more concave in the
case of the male. Colour foods will help to enhance the striking
coloration of these fish. They will take flake food readily and will also eat
various livefood of suitable size.

Rosy tetras are quite active swimmers so their aquarium should have open
areas, with plants being concentrated around the back and sides. Keeping a small shoal of these fish
will give the greatest potential for successful breeding. Choose brightly coloured males and females
which appear plump with spawn.

Raising the temperature slightly in the spawning tank should serve to trigger reproductive activity
within 3 days, with the fry then hatching after a similar interval. Do not leave the adult fish in the
spawning tank, because they will eat the eggs which have been scattered among the vegetation there.

Neon Tetra *(Paracheirodon innesi)*

A shoal of these fish is truly spectacular in a well-planted aquarium, although they can also be kept in the company of other non-aggressive fish of similar size. The neon tetra originates from the Rio Putumayo in eastern Peru and when it first became available to aquarists in 1936, one of these fish would fetch a price equivalent to the average monthly salary at that time. Since then, they have been bred commercially in huge numbers and no longer command a premium price.

Beware of purchasing any neon tetras which show loss of coloration. This is an obvious symptom of the parasitic ailment popularly known as neon tetra disease, although the neon is not the only species which is at risk. Neon tetras will come to the surface to feed on flake food floating there, but they often prefer to seize food in the mid-water area when it is sinking. Invertebrates will be eaten readily.

Once established these tetras can prove long-lived, with a life expectation of a decade or more. Breeding is not too difficult, provided that the spawning tank is kept dark. It is usually possible to differentiate the sexes by the shape of the blue line running down their bodies, since this tends to be straighter and thinner in male neons.

As the pair come together for spawning, the female assumes a near upright position in the water. The eggs then

1in
2.5cm

fall among vegetation, with up to 150 being produced in total. Hatching and rearing details are as for the cardinal tetra (see below).

Cardinal Tetra *(Paracheirodon axelrodi)*

The brilliant colours of cardinal tetras will be emphasized by ensuring optimal water conditions, which will also increase the likelihood of successful breeding. The addition of peat to the aquarium filter will help to create the so-called black water conditions which suit these fish well. This species can be distinguished easily from the neon tetra because of the red stripe that runs down the entire length of its body.

Cardinal tetras show to best effect when kept in shoals. Females in good condition may be recognized by their broader bodies. The addition of livefood to their diet will serve as an important conditioner and will enhance the likelihood of successful breeding. Try to provide terrestrial livefood, such as whiteworm, rather than aquatic livefoods, like tubifex worms, which could introduce disease to the aquarium.

Cardinal tetras scatter their eggs at random and, since these will be eaten in a community aquarium, a special breeding tank is needed. This should be screened and must not be equipped with any lighting because the eggs are sensitive to light. After spawning, the adult fish will need to be removed to prevent them from eating their own eggs. Hatching should take place about a day later, with the fry being free-swimming when they are about 5 days old. Fry food is needed at first for rearing purposes.

2in
5cm

Red Phantom Tetra *(Megalamphodus sweglesi)*

These tetras may be unsuitable for some community aquaria–not because they are aggressive, but because they require a relatively low water temperature of no higher than around 73°F (23°C). Their companions should therefore be chosen with care, but could include species such as the White Cloud Mountain minnow (see page 36) and various dwarf cichlids, with the heaterstat being adjusted accordingly. Regular water changes are also important, to prevent any build-up of nitrates.

Red phantom tetras originate from the upper reaches of the Orinoco River in Colombia. They can be sexed easily because the male fish has a long, red dorsal fin, whereas that of the female is shorter and predominantly blackish, with a white area. Some females also have yellow rather than red markings on their dorsal fin, typically restricted to the base.

Breeding is possible if the water conditions are suitable, with soft, acidic water being vital. Livefood serve as a stimulant for the fish, although they will also eat flake food as a basic diet. Colour food can help to enhance their red coloration. Their eggs are reddish-brown in colour and the fry can be reared on brine shrimp *nauplii* as soon as they are free-swimming, at about 5 days old.

2in
5cm

Black Phantom Tetra *(Megalamphodus megalopterus)*

Occurring further south than its red relative, in parts of Bolivia and Brazil, this tetra has also proved to be more adaptable. It should be housed in a well-planted tank, with floating plants on the surface to ensure diffuse lighting. Be careful when purchasing stock to avoid any in tanks housing thin or sickly individuals, because black phantom tetras are susceptible to piscine tuberculosis. If introduced to an aquarium, this is likely to wipe out the occupants.

Breeding can be accomplished quite easily and males will often display readily, even in the main aquarium. Unusually in this case however, females are more colourful with red adipose fins. The pectoral and anal fins are similarly coloured. The spawning tank should be set up to ensure that the eggs will be protected from light as far as possible, with the bottom and sides being screened. Do not add peat on the floor, because the tannin deposits will make it difficult for the fry to break out of their egg cases. These fish can be reared in a similar way to red phantom tetras.

2in
5cm

Emperor Tetra *(Nematobrycon palmeri)*

The beautiful coloration of the male emperor tetra will be enhanced in an aquarium which is densely planted and has a dark substrate. The upper part of its body shows a distinct violet tinge, with a dark band extending along the flanks. Males tend to be larger than females and their markings are brighter. Another point of distinction is that the dorsal fin is decidedly curved at its tip in male emperor tetras.

It is possible to spawn these tetras, although they are not prolific. The male may drive the female hard, and it is therefore important that both fish are in top breeding condition. The female lays each of her eggs individually, rather than simply releasing a large batch of spawn. Java moss (*Vesicularia dubyana*) makes an ideal spawning medium. Pairs should not be separated once they have spawned successfully, as this should minimise the risk of compatibility problems. Remove the adult fish once spawning is completed, because they will otherwise eat the eggs. Hatching should occur within 2 days, with suitable fry food subsequently being required for the young tetras once they are at the free-swimming stage.

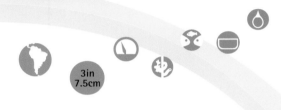

3in
7.5cm

Glass Tetra *(Moenkhausia oligolepis)*

5in
12.5cm

The main area of coloration of these tetras is restricted to the area around their eyes, aside from the black area on the caudal fin. The remainder of their body has a distinct reflective silvery sheen, with the impression of glass being reinforced by their relatively large scales. Glass tetras originate from the Amazon region of Guyana extending into Brazil. They are found in slow moving stretches of water and are active swimmers by nature; unplanted stretches in their aquarium are therefore important. While young glass tetras are quite amenable by nature, large individuals may prey on any small fish sharing their quarters. Large glass tetras should in this case only be accommodated with tank mates of similar size.

Spawning can be achieved without great difficulty; at this stage it is possible to distinguish the sexes as females swell with their eggs. Sources of animal protein, such as freeze-dried tubifex and similar foods, are required for conditioning purposes and need to be offered for several weeks beforehand. The fish can then be moved to a spawning tank once egg laying is imminent.

The female glass tetra lays in vegetation, releasing her eggs in groups of a dozen or so, and darts out afterwards into open water, followed by the male. Several hundred eggs will be produced in this fashion, and they should hatch within 3 days. The fry will be free-swimming in a further 5 days. Fry foods, followed by brine shrimp *nauplii* and similar foods, are recommended for rearing purposes.

Diamond Tetra *(Moenkhausia pittieri)*

This tetra originates from Lake Valencia and adjacent waterways in Venezuela. Its body is entirely silvery, although iridescence creates shades ranging from pale violet through to green, depending on the light. A golden hue may also be apparent in some cases, while there is a distinct red area on the upper part of each eye.

Sexing is not difficult in this case, as the dorsal fin of the male is significantly larger and more curved than that of the female. Like others of its genus, the diamond tetra will not thrive in hard water, or where the concentration of nitrate is allowed to rise in the aquarium. Regular partial water changes will therefore be essential.

Although these tetras can be maintained satisfactorily on flake, they must be offered a range of livefood to condition them for spawning. Mosquito larvae are often favoured for this purpose, especially as large numbers can be cultured easily in relatively sterile surroundings outdoors. The required quantity can then be sieved off and offered to the fish. However, their availability is generally restricted to temperate areas in the summer months.

The spawning habits of the diamond tetra are similar to those of the glass tetra, with as many as 400 eggs being laid. Once the adult fish have been transferred back to their aquarium, raising the temperature in the spawning tank to 79°F (26°C) will speed up the hatching process without harmful effects so the eggs will be less vulnerable to fungal attack.

Disc Tetra *(Poptella orbicularis)*

This fish is sometimes called the salmon discus but it should not be confused with the discus (*Symphysodon aequifasciata*), which is featured on page 69 and is a much larger fish. Disc tetras are found over a wide area of South America, from Guyana to Paraguay. They have a relatively flat yet broad body, which is silvery in colour and iridescent so that, depending on the light, disc tetras may appear to have green, blue, pink or violet suffusions. Two very indistinct bars are apparent on each side of the body behind the gill covers.

Disc tetras are an ideal choice for the larger community aquarium, although they may damage plants and often browse on new shoots which can be particularly infuriating. Vegetable matter in their diet may help to deflect their attention away from the aquarium plants or, alternatively, only include plants which are likely to be ignored, such as Java fern (*Microsorium pteropus*). An aquarium for disc tetras should not be heavily planted in any event, since they are active fish by nature and need plenty of swimming space.

A large spawning tank is essential as the female may produce as many as 2000 eggs. The sexes cannot be distinguished, but the female swells with eggs prior to spawning. A pair will spawn in open water, and marbles on the floor of the aquarium offer some protection for the eggs until the adult fish are removed. The fry will be feeding on brine shrimp *nauplii* by about 6 days old.

Congo Tetra *(Micralestes interruptus)*

These African characins are found in the upper reaches of the River Congo in Zaire. Their coloration is unusual–depending on the angle of the lighting, nearly all the colours of the rainbow seem to become evident–ranging from yellow through shades of red to green, blue and even violet tones. Males typically display the strongest iridescence and are larger in size, with more elaborate fins, than females. Regular partial water changes seem to improve the quality of their finnage.

Congo tetras will eat a range of invertebrates, even tackling white-coated mini mealworms *(Tenebrio molitor)* as well as more conventional fare such as flake, although they are not generally bold feeders. Other fish sharing their quarters may therefore take the pick of the items being offered. These tetras will sometimes eat the plants in their aquarium, but damage is usually sporadic and confined to young shoots.

A pair can usually be persuaded to breed on their own, although Congo tetras appear to spawn in shoals naturally. Their spawning quarters should be planted with fine-leaved vegetation, such as *Myriophyllum*, with the eggs being released here. There may be as many as 300 and spawning usually occurs in the morning, triggered by the early rays of sunshine reaching the tank.

Hatching occurs from 5 days onwards and the young are immediately free-swimming. Rotifers make an ideal first food, with brine shrimp *nauplii* being introduced after the first few days. It is especially important with young Congo tetras to include peat in the aquarium water or they are liable to succumb to fungus. Adult fish will also benefit from this type of environment.

3in
7.5cm

Red-finned Tetra *(Aphyocharax anisitsi)*

This particular tetra is known under a variety of other common names, including the bloodfin and the red-finned characin. It also used to have the scientific name of *A. rubripennis*. Originating from Argentina and Paraguay, the red-finned tetra derives its name from the extensive red markings present on most of its fins, aside from the pectorals which are colourless. The body itself is silvery, with a slight bluish iridescence in some lights.

Some aquarists have suggested that now that it is being commercially bred the red coloration of this fish is not as bright as it used to be, but a varied diet, including colour food and *Daphnia*, should ensure a good depth of colour. It is worth noting that young red-finned tetras actually display very little trace of red on their fins at first.

When catching these fish, always take particular care to check that the hooks present on the anal fins of the male are carefully removed from the net. Otherwise, if these are lost, the male will not be able to grasp the female when mating occurs.

2in
5cm

Shallow water to a depth of no more than 3in (7.5cm), should be provided in their spawning tank, so the eggs can fall quickly through into the protection of a spawning grid on the floor and out of reach of the adult fish which may otherwise eat them. A pair may splash at the surface–this is normal behaviour and is not a reflection of the depth of water.

Red-finned tetras will produce a relatively large number of eggs, often in excess of 750. The young, which hatch about a day later, are not especially difficult to rear, starting on a diet of rotifers once they are free-swimming.

One-striped African Characin *(Nannaethiops unitaeniatus)*

This species is widely distributed, being found in the Niger, Congo and Nile rivers throughout equatorial Africa. As might be expected, it is a fairly adaptable aquarium occupant, although somewhat shy by nature. Its coloration is not especially spectacular, with its upper parts being brownish-olive. A narrow gold stripe and a dark line extend down the sides of the body, with the latter continuing into the caudal fin. The underparts are mainly silvery.

Sexing is only possible during the spawning period, when the male one-striped African characin develops its characteristic red coloration both in the upper part of the caudal fin and in the square-shaped dorsal fin.

The spawning quarters for a pair should be well planted with fine-leaved vegetation such as *Cabomba*. The eggs, numbering as many as 500, will be scattered around the tank, with hatching occurring 2 days later. The fry will start to swim freely around their quarters in a further 5 days, and can be reared quite easily. The rather jerky swimming action of these fish is normal, and not a cause for concern.

3in
7.5cm

X-ray Fish *(Pristella maxillaris)*

1in
2.5cm

The semi-transparent appearance of these fish explains their common name, with the dots running along the sides of the body serving to highlight their vertebral column. The internal organs are concealed in a silvery sac on the lower part of the body. The coloration of their fins will be enhanced if their aquarium has relatively subdued lighting. Sexing is possible when the fish are in a good light, since the swim bladder of the male is significantly more pointed than that of the female when illuminated from behind.

Originating from northern parts of South America these fish are quite easy to maintain, even being found in stretches of brackish water in the wild, and they can be kept in a similar aquarium environment if acclimatized accordingly. A varied diet and an open area for swimming are recommended.

Breeding is also quite straightforward once a compatible pair has been recognized. Spawning will take place among plants, with a female laying as many as 400 eggs in total. Hatching takes place about a day later, and the tiny fry will subsequently need to be fed a suitable rearing food. As they grow, partial water changes must be carried out frequently.

Blind Cave Fish *(Astyanax fasciatus mexicanus)*

These remarkable fish originate from a network of underground caves in Mexico, where they have lost their eyesight and pigmentation–although their body retains a pinkish sheen. These adaptations to a subterranean existence do not disadvantage them, and normal individuals occur in some rivers elsewhere in the country.

Blind cave fish actually hatch with eyes but as they become older skin starts to cover the surface of their eyes. In a dark environment, where eyesight would be of little value, blind cave fish rely for information on their lateral lines, which are the sensory canals running down each side of the body that detect vibrations in the water. These enable them to find food easily while avoiding obstructions and predators. Blind cave fish can sometimes prove rather troublesome in a community aquarium as they may nip the fins of their companions. They are active fish by nature.

Subdued lighting and a cave-like decor, which can be made using securely fixed pieces of slate, can provide a striking and unusual replica of the native world of these fish in the aquarium.

Spawning of this species is fairly easy. The female will swell with eggs, which is the only obvious way of sexing. The male will display by swimming around her until the time for spawning occurs. He then moves in and swims very close to his mate so he can fertilize her eggs as she releases them. Remove the fish, or their eggs if they spawn in the main aquarium, as, in spite of their lack of vision, they will easily locate and eat their eggs.

4in
10cm

Marbled Headstander *(Abramites hypselonotus)*

There can be confusion concerning the name of this American characin, which is also known as the high-backed headstander (*A. microcephalus*). In common with other fish of its kind, it rests with its nose pointed downwards, at an angle of about 45°. The basic coloration of the marbled headstander is striped, with a series of broad brown bands crossing its body. The fins are essentially free from pigmentation, aside from the brown pelvic fin and brown coloration on part of the dorsal fin.

Found in the waters of the Orinoco and Amazon, the marbled headstander requires an aquarium decorated with rockwork and submerged wood. Only tough plants should be included, because these fish will eat vegetation. Substitute sources of green food such as spinach or lettuce can be provided, taking care to ensure that any left uneaten will not pollute the aquarium. A vegetable flake food can be used as a regular diet and the addition of spirulina could also be useful.

Marbled headstanders will swim near the surface and can jump. Care needs to be taken therefore, especially when attempting to catch them, to prevent the fish leaping out of the tank. This is not a species that will breed readily in aquarium surroundings.

5in
12.5cm

Spotted Headstander *(Chilodus punctatus)*

These attractively marked headstanders originate from northern parts of
South America, including Guyana. Some individuals may have a more
golden hue to their silvery body coloration. The characteristic dark spots cover the body, although the fins are
relatively clear–apart from the tall dorsal fin, which
is often spotted or may even be blotched with
black markings.

Spotted headstanders acquired a reputation for being
rather delicate in the past, but in a well-maintained
aquarium their care now poses no particular problems.
They will not thrive in brightly lit surroundings however, and may refuse to feed. Their diet should consist
both of vegetable matter, which can be in the form of
prepared foods as well as fresh items, and livefood.

The onset of spawning activity results in the loss of the
spotted markings. These are then replaced by large black
patches, about the size of peas, behind each eye. The eggs are
laid among vegetation such as Java moss (*Vesicularia
dubyana*). The fry will be free-swimming within 5 days of
hatching and can be reared on small livefood such as brine shrimp
nauplii. They adopt the characteristic headstanding posture even at
this early stage in life. In order to ensure successful hatching, water
conditions must be good, although it has proved possible on occasions
to release fry alive from their egg cases by carefully cutting through
the membrane with a scalpel.

4in
10cm

Striped Anostomus *(Anostomus anostomus)*

7in
18cm

The streamlined,
torpedo-like body shape of
these fish helps them to swim in the
relatively fast flowing areas of water
which they inhabit in northern South
America. A power filter in their aquarium
will serve to replicate these surroundings. The
protruding lower jaw of the striped anostomus allows it to
browse on algae, effectively feeding upside down. Rockwork in
the aquarium will not only provide it with retreats, but is also a
suitable medium for algal growth.

It is preferable not to accommodate striped anostomus alongside other algal eating species, such as the Siamese flying fox
(*Epalzeorhynchus siamensis*), since their method of feeding tends
to put them at a disadvantage. Aside from vegetable-based foods

such as spirulina, striped anostomus will
also eat small livefood readily.
Striped anostomus are not
especially social with others
of their own kind. If two
individuals are kept
one is almost
inevitably likely to
be bullied by its
companion, whereas with a larger group, in a suitably spacious
aquarium, outbreaks of aggression tend to be less severe.
Adequate retreats such as rocks and submerged wood should be
included in their tank. It is difficult to sex these fish visually,
although the red markings on the fins tend to be brighter in
males. Successful breeding in aquarium surroundings is an
exceedingly rare event.

Golden Pencilfish *(Nannostomus beckfordi)*

The generic name *Nannostomus* means 'small mouth', and this is reflected by the diet which these fish require. They can be offered flake food and only the smallest livefood such as *Daphnia* and *Cyclops*. In a community aquarium, pencilfish are likely to be among the last fish to eat, so a watch should be kept on them to ensure they are receiving sufficient food.

There can be considerable variation in the coloration of the golden pencilfish. Some individuals are of a much redder shade than others, which is why this species is rather confusingly known as the red pencilfish as well. As the time for spawning approaches, the abdomen of the male fish assumes a particularly rich red appearance. The shape of the anal fin can be used at other times to determine the gender of an individual, being round in shape at the front in the case of a male, and straight-edged and pointed in the female.

Raising the water temperature to 86°F (30°C) may help to encourage spawning activity. Golden pencilfish lay their eggs within clumps of fine-leaved plants such as *Myriophyllum*. Water conditions should be similar to those for other

South American characins from the northern part of the continent. Relatively few eggs are produced at a spawning and these are likely to be avidly consumed by the adult fish, which must therefore be removed as soon as possible afterwards. Infusoria or a suitable commercial fry food should be used for rearing purposes.

Three-lined Pencilfish *(Nannostomus trifasciatus)*

Not to be confused with the two-lined species (*N. bifasciatus*), these pencilfish can be distinguished by the black bands extending along the back, side and underparts of their body. Interestingly, at night these bands are replaced by dark markings running across rather than along the fish's body. The difference in the shape of the anal fins can again be used to separate the sexes, and females may also have a more rounded body shape.

Depending on their origins, there may be some natural variation in the colour of these fish. Some appear to have

much redder areas on the fins and this feature is often combined with a broader dark central stripe. Although introduced to the hobby as long ago as 1912, the three-lined pencilfish has never been especially common, although it is an attractive fish which shows to good effect in groups.

Unfortunately, these pencilfish have proved to be difficult to spawn, and are not prolific. Their fry hatch within 2 days and are free-swimming by a week old. Infusoria makes a suitable first food, while adults can be fed on powdered flake food as well as small livefood.

Silver Hatchetfish *(Gasteropelecus sternicia)*

All hatchetfish have a particularly deep body and a fairly flat dorsal profile with an upturned mouth. They spend much of their time close to the surface of the water. Their aquarium should be covered because they are actually able to glide for distances above the water using their pectoral fins to keep themselves airborne. They have been known to travel up to 4ft (1.2m) in the wild in this fashion.

The silver hatchetfish is the largest species, and a school will make an impressive sight in the aquarium. Their care is relatively straightforward and they will eat a range of floating foods, including flake, although insects such as wingless fruit flies or even hatchling crickets should be offered when available.

It is possible to sex these hatchetfish, since the females have a more rounded keel when viewed from the front and, when mature, they are also larger than males. Very little has been recorded about their breeding habits. Eggs may be deposited among vegetation, with several hundred being produced at a single spawning. The fry of hatchetfish have been successfully reared on rotifers and *Cyclops nauplii* at first.

3in
7.5cm

Marbled Hatchetfish *(Carnegiella strigata)*

The striking silvery-white and variable dark areas on the body of these hatchetfish is responsible for their common name. They originate from northern South America and, like other hatchet-fish, require a fairly spacious aquarium in view of their active nature. Their sleek body shape means they can remain almost stationary as well, even in powerful currents.

Marbled hatchetfish require a diet based on small inverte-brates such as wingless fruit flies *(Drosophila)*. *Drosophila* cultures are available from specialist suppliers advertising in the fishkeeping magazines. The flies themselves can be bred easily and reared on special foods or even old banana skins. Small aquatic livefood, such as *Daphnia* or mosquito larvae, are an alternative food. Flake food will be eaten but, for breeding purposes in particular, livefood is essential. The best time to feed marbled hatchetfish is towards dusk, when they naturally become more active.

When purchasing these and other hatchetfish, look carefully for signs of white spot (see page 21). They are susceptible to this parasitic disease, and new stock must always be quarantined to avoid any risk of introducing it to an established aquarium. The stress of a move may trigger an outbreak in what appears to be healthy stock. Discard the water in the bag, so as to minimise the risk of the development of these parasites, rather than tipping it into the quarantine tank. Breeding details are similar to those of the previous species and peat extract can serve as a conditioner. Fry hatch after a day or so and will be swimming freely in a further 5 days.

2in
5cm

Six-barred Distichodus *(Distichodus sexfasciatus)*

Originating from the equatorial region of Africa, these characins are distinctly marked with six black bands on each side of their body when young. These markings fade as the fish grow older however, and become greyer in coloration. The orange-tan areas are also affected.

While young six-barred distichodus make attractive occupants of a community aquarium, they are likely to outgrow their accommodation in due course. These fish are active by nature and require plenty of clear water for swimming. Unfortunately, they are likely to damage

plants growing in the aquarium and plastic substitutes are a better option. One plant which is usually robust enough to avoid their attention is Java fern (*Microsorium pteropus*), and this can be grown on bogwood or other tank decor such as slate.

Fresh greenstuff should feature regularly in the diet of six-barred distichodus, along with other items such as rolled oats. Prepared vegetarian foods, including spirulina, will be eaten, as well as small invertebrates such as *Daphnia* on occasions. Breeding these fish in aquarium surroundings is exceedingly unlikely, particularly as there is no clear visual way of distinguishing the sexes; they would be most likely to spawn in a pond in a tropical house.

12in
30cm

Silver Distichodus *(Distichodus affinis)*

This distichodus is far less streamlined than the preceding species. It originates from the same part of Africa however, and requires similar care. In fact, it is much easier to house a shoal of these fish in an aquarium because they will attain a significantly smaller adult size than the six-barred form. One of the distinguishing feature of the silver distichodus is its divided, rounded tail fin. There is a black area on the dorsal fin, blackish markings on the sides of the body and a reddish suffusion to the fins.

It is not always easy to identify these distichodus with certainty however, because a number of similar fish are known. In comparison with Nobol's distichodus (*D. noboli*), for example, the relative lengths of the dorsal and anal fins provide a means of distinction, with the dorsal being longer in the case of silver distichodus. Young fish tend to be much paler in coloration, being mainly silver, often with a slight pink suffusion on the belly.

The general care of the silver distichodus should be similar to that of the six-barred distichodus. They can be kept with others which are likely to destroy vegetation and require similar water conditions.

7in
18cm

Red-bellied Piranha *(Serrasalmus nattereri)*

This is probably the most common species of these notorious fish likely to be encountered in aquatic circles, although in some parts of the world they are banned because of fears they could be deliberately released and become established in the wild. The red-bellied piranha naturally occurs over a wide area of South America, from Guyana south to the La Plata region of Argentina.

Young piranhas of this species are silvery with relatively transparent fins and slight dark spots visible on their flanks. Even at this stage their lower jaw protrudes and teeth are present in the mouth. Old individuals are darker, with iridescence apparent over much of the body and a reddish underside.

As aquarium occupants, piranhas have quite specific requirements. Although it may be possible to keep a group of young piranhas together, a smaller individual may be bullied and attacked, or even killed. They need a large aquarium and a powerful filtration system, which will also serve to create a current in the water. Feeding meat rapidly pollutes the water, especially if any is left uneaten, and prepared alternatives will provide a more balanced diet in any event.

Breeding has been achieved in large aquaria, with females being recognizable by their more yellowish coloration. As many as 1000 eggs may be laid after a fairly aggressive spawning encounter. The young fry can be reared on brine shrimps at first; they will need to be split into groups of similar size as they grow, to prevent cannibalism.

12in
30cm

Black-finned Pacu *(Colossoma oculus)*

Although the general appearance of these fish resembles that of piranhas, they are far less aggressive in their feeding habits. They may eat smaller companions, but they are primarily vegetarian in their feeding habits. Young pacus, just a few inches long, are very attractive in appearance, with silvery coloration on their flanks along with dark spots and reddish markings on the belly and fins.

These fish grow quickly and will soon need larger accommodation. They are not a species to select unless you are ultimately prepared to invest in a large and well-filtered set-up for them. Pacus are better kept in groups of three or four, as solitary individuals are often very nervous. There should be adequate retreats within the aquarium for them.

16in
40cm

The coloration of these pacus will darken significantly as they grow older, becoming blackish. A varied diet comprising fresh greenstuff, such as garden peas, and herbivorous food sticks should be provided. Black-finned pacus prefer to feed at the surface, and have healthy appetites. Breeding is unlikely to be accomplished with any success in the aquarium, although males may be distinguished from females by the more pointed appearance of their dorsal fin. Poor water quality will soon lead to obvious signs of ragged fins in black-finned pacus however, which makes sexing impossible.

Silver Dollar *(Metynnis argenteus)*

The rounded, coin-like shape of this fish has led to its common name. Its silvery body may have occasional black spots distributed over the surface, which enables individuals to be recognized easily. A small group make an attractive addition to an aquarium of other characins from this part of the world. Unfortunately, as with other *Metynnis* species, they will eat vegetation growing in their tank and it may be wise to use plastic plants for this reason.

Fresh greenstuff should feature in their diet. Food such as cress can be easily cultivated in small amounts on a windowsill for this purpose, even if you do not have access to a garden. Small amounts can be cut when needed and there is no worry with such foods that they might have been treated with chemicals which might harm the fish. It has been suggested that male silver dollars can be recognized by the presence of a red area just in front of their anal fin, which is also longer than in the case of females. Females will lay as many as 2000 eggs, which will start to hatch after 3 days.

8in
20cm

Fanning Characin *(Pyrrhulina rachoviana)*

3in
7.5cm

The small size of this fish means that it should not be kept with larger companions which might even inadvertently harass it. These characins show to best effect in groups. Pairs can be identified quite easily, since mature males have significantly redder anal and caudal fins than females.

Fanning characins are easy to maintain on a diet of flake and livefood of suitable size, such as microworms; livefood is especially important as a conditioner for breeding purposes. The spawning habits of these fish is particularly fascinating. It is important that the spawning tank is covered and that the water level is significantly lower than the top. The pair will spawn out of the water, with the eggs being deposited on the glass or a leaf, in clumps of perhaps 10 or so, in a very short space of time.

In total, up to 200 eggs may be laid in this way. The male will then prevent the eggs from dessicating by splashing them repeatedly with his fins until they hatch. This occurs about a day or so later, and the young fish will then begin to feed on special fry food within a couple of days.

Spraying Characin *(Copeina arnoldi)*

This fish is now considered to be a separate species from the fanning characin (*Pyrrhulina rachoviana*), although their appearance and habits are very similar. The spraying characin originates from the lower reaches of the Amazon. Males are significantly larger in size than females and look rather like miniature sharks.

As the time for spawning approaches the female will swell with her ova, developing a more rounded shape as a result. This is the stage to transfer the fish to the spawning tank. A piece of slate is traditionally provided for spawning purposes; it should be firmly set in place with part of the rock protruding at an angle above the water's surface. In due course, the rock will be inspected by the male; ultimately, the pair will leap out of the water together and lie briefly

on the rock, where spawning occurs, before they slide back underwater. It can take up to one and a half hours for the full complement of eggs to be laid in this way. The eggs will be laid in batches and the male will again splash them repeatedly, using his tail to keep them moist. Once the fry hatch, they will drop out of sight to the bottom of the tank. At this stage, the adult spraying characins should be transferred back to their own aquarium.

Red-spotted Characin *(Copeina guttata)*

Males are well marked with red spots during the spawning season, while females have far fewer spots and are paler in overall coloration. These fish are found in the central part of the Amazon basin. They are active fish, in spite of their small size, and feed largely on livefood, although they will also take flake food.

Red-spotted characins will spawn in the substrate of their quarters, and may disturb the planting arrangements at this stage; at all other times, they will ignore the vegetation in their tank. The use of coarse sand on the floor of a spawning tank may be better than gravel so that the fish can excavate a depression, using their fins and heads, for their eggs more easily. After the female spawns, the male fertilizes the eggs and transfers them to the pit on his anal fin. As many as 2500 eggs may be produced in succession as a result of a single spawning. The male will then drive the female away and she should be transferred back to the main aquarium. Once the eggs start to hatch, after a day or so, he too can be removed, or he might start to eat his offspring. A fry food, followed by brine shrimps, can be used for rearing.

6in
15cm

Penguin Fish *(Thayeri boehlkei)*

The distinctive black and yellowish-silver coloration of these fish is the reason for their common name. The black stripe running down the sides of their body extends into the lower part of the caudal fin. This serves to separate this species from the closely-related form known as *T. obliqua*, which is also called the penguin fish but has its black stripe restricted to the rear part of the body.

Water quality is especially significant in the case of penguin fish, with regular partial changes being carried out. It is quite normal for these fish to swim with their heads directed upwards in the water, but this is not a cause for concern. Penguin fish will eat both flake and livefood, including freeze-dried items such as tubifex.

Sexing is not possible visually outside the breeding season, although at this stage, the females become more rounded in appearance. Once established, pairs should be kept together if possible, since spawning then tends to be more reliable. However, this may not always be practical if a group of these fish are being housed in a community aquarium.

These characins simply spawn in water, with females producing as many as 1000 eggs. The fish should then be returned to their aquarium. The water in the spawning tank should be partially changed at this stage, as the male's large volume of sperm will rapidly deteriorate and pollute the water. The fry start to hatch within a day, and are free-swimming about 4 days later.

Long-finned Characin *(Alestes longipennis)*

Originating from tropical West Africa, this species is so named because of the elongated rays on the dorsal fin of males. Their overall coloration can vary from shades of yellow-green to olive-green, with a silvery iridescence also being apparent. There is a reddish-orange area above the eye and a prominent black streak close to the caudal fin which extends into it.

Long-finned characins will thrive in a well-planted aquarium which is not brightly lit. Their rather nervous nature will cause them to attempt to leap out of the water if frightened, and their aquarium must be covered as a precaution. Regular water changes are essential to prevent any accumulation of nitrates.

Although these characins can be kept as part of a mixed aquarium, it is essential to have a group for breeding purposes because they spawn communally. Each female may lay 300 or more eggs, typically among fine-leaved plants to which the eggs will stick. The addition of live-food to their regular diet of flake food will encourage breeding activity. Hatching may take as long as 6 days, with the young initially feeding on rotifers.

CICHLIDS

O ften described as fish with personality, members of this group attract a strong following in spite of the fact that many cichlids are not suitable for community aquaria and need to be kept on their own, especially as they grow larger. These fish can prove to be disruptive in aquaria, often digging in the substrate and uprooting any plants. They are also likely to be territorial.

Cichlids can be broadly divided into two categories. There are those occurring in the Americas, including the popular discus and angelfish, and others from Africa. Those found in the lakes of the Rift valley area of eastern Africa have very specific requirements in terms of water chemistry. Asiatic cichlids are significantly fewer in number, and less commonly kept, although their care presents no particular problems. In some parts of Asia, these fish are found in brackish water.

Oscar *(Astronotus ocellatus)*

This is one of the most popular and widely kept cichlids today, although it is important to bear in mind that the young fish often offered for sale will grow into relatively large adults and will require suitably spacious accommodation. Oscars can be tamed quite easily and will soon learn to feed from the hand. They are particularly fond of livefood and will also prey on smaller fish, so any companions must be chosen carefully.

12in
30cm

These fish originate from the Amazon region, extending as far south as the Rio Paraguay. They were first introduced to the aquarium hobby in 1929 and since then a number of different colour varieties have been developed. While the wild form of the oscar is a relatively dull coloured fish, with brown blotches and rust-coloured markings, selective breeding has given rise to the tiger or red oscar, which is much more striking with predominantly reddish-orange flanks. There is now also a patterned variety, described as the marble, where there are reddish streaks set against a dark background. The white form of the oscar is also popular. The dark but not the reddish pigment has been lost in this case.

Ideally, an aquarium for oscars should have a sandy bottom. Only tough plants should be included and these should be set in pots because of the way in which these fish will dig into the substrate. Clean flowerpots or slate should be provided as spawning surfaces. Oscars are mature once they are about 4.5in (11cm) long, but they are very difficult to sex until the female is approaching spawning condition. She will then develop swellings around the genital opening.

Nearly 3000 eggs may be laid at a time, with the adult fish then watching over them until they hatch about 3 days later. The fry will be chaperoned into a pit in the sand and they will remain here until they are able to swim freely. The young oscars can be reared on *Cyclops* and similar foods at first.

Ram Cichlid *(Papiliochromis ramirezi)*

Originating from Colombia and western parts of
Venezuela, this colourful cichlid used to be
classified for many years in the genus
Apistogramma. It is also sometimes known as
the butterfly dwarf cichlid. Today's aquarium
strains tend to be more colourful than the
native form and a golden variety has also been
developed. Sexing is straightforward as males
have a much more pronounced dorsal fin, while
females have a reddish tinge to their bellies and
are smaller in size.

  Males should be kept apart from each other in
aquarium surroundings as they are territorial by
nature. Both densely planted and open areas
need to be present in their tank, with the water
being filtered through peat to soften and acidify it. Feeding presents no particular
difficulty, as both sinking foods and
various forms of livefood will be
eaten readily by these cichlids.

  The female may produce up to 200 eggs
at a single spawning. These will often be
laid on the underside of rockwork such as
slate, and are red in colour. Hatching occurs up to 4 days
later and then the fry will be guarded for a week or so by the

female, although not all display such
strong maternal instincts. Repeated
spawning every month or so may be
anticipated, but rams are relatively short-lived with a life
expectancy unlikely to exceed three years.

3in
7.5cm

Agassiz's Dwarf Cichlid *(Apistogramma agassizi)*

Sexing these attractive cichlids presents no difficulties, since
males are significantly more colourful with more elaborate fins.
The tail of the female is also rounded, rather than elongated. A
male can be housed with one or more females in an aquarium
where there are plenty of retreats. Regular water changes, to
prevent an accumulation of nitrates, are important.

Upturned flowerpots are ideal spawning sites for these
cichlids but avoid any which have been used previously and
could have been exposed to chemicals. These cichlids are very
susceptible to pollutants in the water of their aquarium, and
may even react badly to medication, so any treatments must be
used with caution.

The female lays her eggs on
the underside of the flowerpot,
guarding them until the fry
hatch. She then takes care of
them for the first few days
after hatching, with the young
cichlids responding to her
movements as she swims
around the aquarium. This
behaviour is fascinating to
observe and since these
cichlids can be
persuaded to
spawn quite
readily the chances of
breeding success are
relatively high.

3in
7.5cm

Three-striped Dwarf Cichlid *(Apistogramma trifasciata)*

It is not always easy to distinguish the characteristic stripes of these cichlids–especially in females, which have duller coloration than males. The broad black stripe running down the centre of the body to the caudal fin is the most evident. Another stripe extends beneath the dorsal fin, while the third connects the pectoral and anal fins on the lower side of the

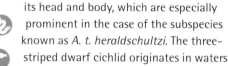
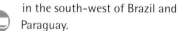

body. The rays just after the front of the dorsal fin and on the pelvic fin are elongated in the case of the male.

This particular cichlid is sometimes called the blue apistogramma because of the blue markings on its head and body, which are especially prominent in the case of the subspecies known as *A. t. heraldschultzi*. The three-striped dwarf cichlid originates in waters in the south-west of Brazil and Paraguay.

Livefood of various types should form the bulk of the diet of this particular cichlid, but in some cases live *Daphnia* may not always be eaten. Instead, they can evoke a maternal instinct in the female fish, which chaperone them like fry. For breeding purposes, each female will require a territory of about 8 sq. in (20 sq. cm) and a single male can be housed with up to four partners in suitably spacious surroundings. Breeding details are similar to those of other *Apistogramma* species, with their eggs being laid in a cave.

Crested Dwarf Cichlid *(Apistogramma cacatuoides)*

The extended rays, which resemble a crest and run along the dorsal fin of these fish, explain why they are also known as cockatoo dwarf cichlids. Distinctive red and black markings are present on the caudal fin, which is not forked in the case of the male. The coloration of these fish can vary, and probably reflects their region of origin. Females may also become more colourful when caring for their offspring, often turning yellow.

Crested dwarf cichlids should be accommodated in the same way as related *Apistogramma* species, in groups comprising one male and several females. The fish tend to swim at different levels in the aquarium, with the male preferring to occupy the upper part while the females stay closer to the floor. Spawning sites need to be evenly spread through the tank, with the females establishing their individual territories around them. Once the fry have hatched, it is not uncommon for them to transfer from their mother to another female. This particular species originates from the upper reaches of the Amazon region, in Peru.

Nijssen's Dwarf Cichlid *(Apistogramma nijsseni)*

This is one of the smaller members of the *Apistogramma* genus and it is found over a wide area of South America. There is often quite significant variation in coloration between individuals, with a red edge to the caudal fin being common. Some barring may be apparent on the flanks, with females being duller in terms of their coloration. Nijssen's dwarf cichlids tend to be more omnivorous in their feeding habits than some other related species, although livefood of various types should still feature prominently in their diet.

Suitable retreats for spawning purposes are again essential. Although less commonly used now, coconut shells with holes drilled into them to allow the fish to enter were used with great success in the past. There is a risk today, however, that these could have been contaminated with potentially harmful chemical residues which might dissolve into the water. Infusoria or a similar substitute should be offered as a first food to the fry once they are swimming with their mother.

2in
5cm

Golden-eyed Dwarf Cichlid *(Nannacara anomala)*

Golden-eyed dwarf cichlids tend to be golden-brown across the back with bluish-green markings apparent on their flanks, although their coloration can vary significantly with darker markings sometimes becoming evident. Their eyes are golden, as their name suggests. Females can be distinguished quite easily by their predominantly yellowish appearance, although they frequently display dark markings as the time for spawning approaches. They are also much smaller than males.

These cichlids are very similar to the *Apistogramma* species in their requirements. They feed almost exclusively on livefood, although they will feed on safer substitutes such as freeze-dried tubifex. Their accommodation should incorporate a range of retreats and

3in
7.5cm

spawning occurs in secluded cave-like surroundings, with up to 300 eggs being produced.

If the aquarium is suitably spacious, more than one female can be kept in the company of a single male and under these conditions the male is less likely to harass a female after she has laid. However, should he prove to be disruptive he will need to be transferred elsewhere, leaving her to care for the fry once they hatch. A suitable fry food or infusoria should be used at first for them.

Flag Cichlid *(Laetacara curviceps)*

The shape of this fish's head has led to it also being known as the sheepshead acara, with *Acara* being its old generic name; these cichlids have also been classified in the *Aequidens* genus. They occur in streams running through the Amazon basin. Sexing presents no particular problem as males are bigger and have elongated dorsal and anal fins. Their coloration can vary quite widely, but they generally have a silvery tone with yellow evident on the flanks and blue markings extending into the fins.

    Livefood should feature prominently in their diet, although they will also consume flake food on occasions. Flag cichlids are vulnerable to cloudiness of the cornea; this is caused by 'old' water in the aquarium which contains a relatively high level of nitrate. In severe cases, this may cause their eyes to protrude from the sockets. Carry out partial water changes regularly therefore, to prevent problems of this kind.

    When the time for spawning approaches, these cichlids can become disruptive and should be moved to a separate tank. Their eggs are likely to be laid on rockwork, or possibly broad-leaved plants. The adult fish guard the eggs until they hatch about 3 days later. Once the young are free-swimming, after a similar interval, they can be reared on brine shrimp *nauplii*. They grow quickly if well fed, and may be 0.5in (1.25cm) long by the time they are a month old.

Blue Acara *(Aequidens pulcher)*

These attractive cichlids originate from Panama and northern South America, including the island of Trinidad. Sexing can be problematical in the case of fish which are not in top condition because the pointed tips to the caudal and anal fins, which would indicate a male, may be less evident than normal.

    The basic body coloration of the blue acara is actually yellowish-brown, with a series of up to eight dark vertical stripes encompassing the body. Blue, or bluish-green, spots and streaks are evident on the body, extending across the fins in some cases. There is likely to be a yellowish-red border to the dorsal fin. This species can also sometimes be known as *A. latifrons*.

    Good water quality is essential to maintain these fish in top condition and about one third of the water in their aquarium should be changed every seven to ten days. Although they will not destroy plants growing in their quarters, being essentially insectivorous in their feeding habits, blue acaras will excavate in the aquarium substrate and it may be better to keep plants in pots.

    These cichlids have proved to be one of the easier members of the genus to breed successfully and they develop strong pair bonds. The female usually lays on rockwork or slate, making no attempt to conceal the eggs. Rearing of the fry is relatively straightforward and the young blue acaras will themselves be mature once they reach about 2.5in (7cm) long.

Brown Acara *(Aequidens portalegrensis)*

This particular cichlid, which occurs in southern parts of Brazil, as well as in Paraguay and Bolivia, is known under a wide variety of common names. These include black, green, and port acara. They are easy to keep and spawn readily, provided that a pair is obtained in the first instance. While males tend to display a green iridescence, females may have a redder or more brownish appearance. As the time for spawning approaches both sexes turn black.

6in
15cm

The brown acara will disrupt the floor covering in the aquarium by burrowing, so it may be better just to include floating plants in the tank and leave a plain gravel base. Livefood, including freeze-dried items, should feature prominently in their diet, although these cichlids may sometimes eat flake food.

Brown acaras will spawn on rockwork, with up to 500 eggs being laid by the female. A pair usually prove to be dedicated parents, to the extent that they can be left with their fry. They may even spawn again as their brood grows older, although repeated spawning is more likely when the young are transferred elsewhere after a couple of weeks or so.

Keyhole Cichlid *(Aequidens maronii)*

The coloration of this cichlid is relatively subdued, being predominantly brownish. A dark stripe runs through the eye and the characteristic key-shaped marking, which is especially prominent in young individuals, is present on the upper part of the body, below the dorsal fin. A pinkish hue may be evident, typically along the underpart of the body. These cichlids tend to darken in colour if upset.

Keyhole cichlids are found in the waters of Guyana and Surinam in northern South America. Males can be identified by the trailing rays towards the rear of the dorsal fin, with the anal fin being similarly elongated. In contrast to most cichlids, which tend to be rather bold fish by nature, this particular species is rather shy and retiring. Breeding is also more difficult to achieve than in the case of others of this genus.

An aquarium for keyhole cichlids must include plenty of retreats. Plants can usually be included since they are unlikely to destroy or uproot them, even when spawning. These cichlids will eat a varied diet, although livefood again should predominate whether fresh or in other forms such as freeze-dried.

The rock chosen as the spawning site is typically flat and slate is ideal for this purpose. Up to 300 eggs may be laid and the young cichlids are guarded by their parents, sometimes remaining together as a group for up to 6 months.

4in
10cm

Checkerboard Cichlid *(Crenicara filamentosa)*

These colourful cichlids are thought to originate from the central Amazon region. It is possible to sex them quite easily once they are mature, since adult females have red ventral fins. A clear indicator of spawning condition is the appearance of a broken black band running down the middle of the sides of the body.

Unlike many cichlids, members of the *Crenicara* genus will lay their eggs on the leaves of plants in the aquarium, such as cryptocorynes. The male loses his bright coloration and clamps his fins at this stage, which may make him look decidedly ill, but this is quite normal.

The female will produce up to 100 eggs and she will assume responsibility for their care. This tends to be short-lived however, and after a day or so the spawning plant should be transferred to a tank with fresh water where the fry will start to hatch about two and a half days after egg laying. Tiny rotifers make an ideal starter food when the fry become free-swimming in a further 4 days. Regular daily water changes appear to be essential for their wellbeing.

3in
7.5cm

Texas Cichlid *(Herichthys cyanoguttatum)*

This is a relatively hardy cichlid, originating from the state of Texas in the USA southwards to the north-eastern part of Mexico. It has a brownish-green background colour with bluish-white blotches, although some individuals have a stronger bluish coloration overall. Characteristic irregular black blotches are apparent on the flanks. As these fish mature, males tend to develop a characteristic hump on their heads and may also be more brightly coloured.

The Texas cichlid is sometimes confused with another species known as the blue Texas cichlid (*Cichlasoma carpinte*), which also occurs in Mexico. In this case however, the fins are decidedly blue in colour rather than being relatively translucent. Both species are similar in their behaviour and requirements.

These cichlids have bold and potentially aggressive natures, being highly territorial. They will also seek to rearrange the decor in their aquarium, so it needs to be robust and firmly supported. A varied diet, with the emphasis on livefood, is needed.

Pairs must be kept separate for spawning purposes. The eggs are laid on a rock which the female diligently cleans beforehand. Once the fry hatch, they are transferred to spawning pits dug by the female. It may be better to move some fry to a separate tank because not all pairs prove to be reliable parents.

12in
30cm

Jack Dempsey Cichlid *(Cichlasoma octofasciatum)*

This pugnacious cichlid has the unique distinction of being named after the famous boxer, reflecting its aggressive characteristics. It naturally occurs in Central America, being found in slow flowing stretches of water in the Yucatan province of Mexico, as well as Guatemala and Honduras. Mature males are significantly brighter in colour than females, and have pointed dorsal and anal fins.

Jack Dempsey cichlids will soon uproot and often eat plants in their aquarium but, in their favour, they are quite colourful and easy to keep. They will take a variety of foods, often preferring crustaceans such as shrimps. Breeding is also quite easy to achieve, in a tank which includes rockwork for spawning purposes.

Females are likely to lay about 500 eggs, although larger numbers are sometimes recorded. They are mature by about 5in (13cm) long and subsequently raising the temperature of the water slightly can serve to trigger breeding activity. Hatching will then occur about 3 days later and the fry will be watched over by both parents. They should be separated when they begin to develop their dark stripes.

8in
20cm

Firemouth Cichlid *(Cichlasoma meeki)*

This is one of the most colourful Central America cichlids found in Guatemala and Mexico. The fiery red coloration is present on the lower part of the body and especially prominent on the sides of the face. Males are particularly brightly coloured and have impressive extensions to their dorsal and anal fins. The remainder of the body is brownish with dark spots on the flanks which may form more obvious stripes. Blue markings are apparent on the dorsal fin in particular.

Firemouth cichlids are relatively peaceful by nature, although they are likely to become aggressive as the time for spawning approaches. They can be fed a variety of prepared foods, although bloodworms are often a favourite.

These cichlids prefer an aquarium with a sandy rather than gravel base. Any plants here should be kept in pots as they may be uprooted during spawning, although the eggs themselves are laid on slate in the typical fashion of this group of cichlids. As part of its display, the male firemouth cichlid will inflate its throat sac and open its gill cover. This is quite normal behaviour and not indicative of any health problem.

Up to 500 eggs may be laid, with the fry being shepherded into pits in the substrate by the adult cichlids. As soon as they are free-swimming, they can be offered brine shrimp *nauplii*. Subsequently, colour food may serve to improve the depth of their red coloration. Today's domesticated strains tend to be more brightly coloured than the wild form of this cichlid.

6in
15cm

Midas Cichlid *(Cichlasoma citrinellum)*

The midas cichlid, so called because of its golden colour, ranges from southern Mexico down to Nicaragua. Mature males of this species are particularly impressive with their long, flowing dorsal and anal fins and the pronounced nuchal hump present on their head. Unfortunately, they are aggressive fish by this stage and a male will not hesitate to attack his intended partner should she reject his advances.

It is possible to see by close examination when a female is likely to spawn, as small projections known as breeding tubes can be seen on the underside of the body between the ventral and anal fins. Even with an established pair, courtship can be a turbulent period with the fish often anchoring on to each other's fins in typical cichlid fashion. It is important to keep a watch on the fish at this stage, and to separate them for a period if necessary, to prevent the female being badly injured.

Tank decor should be kept to a minimum and it may well be safer to rely on an external heat source. Rockwork provided as a spawning surface must be firmly supported. The eggs are watched over by the adult fish and although signs of fungus will crop up on those which are infertile this should not be a cause for concern. Those fry which hatch will be kept in pits until they are swimming freely at about a week old. Young midas cichlids are brown in colour, with blackish markings.

12in
30cm

Festive Cichlid *(Mesonauta festiva)*

This cichlid used to be classified in the *Cichlasoma* genus and is also known as the flag cichlid. It is found in relatively slow flowing waters in the northern part of South America, where there is plenty of vegetative cover. A similar planting scheme in the aquarium will suit these fish well with emphasis being placed on relatively tough plants, including *Vallisneria* species and various cryptocorynes. Bogwood can also be added, and some slate will serve to encourage egg laying.

Unfortunately, it is difficult to sex these cichlids visually–although males can often be identified by their elongated dorsal fin. Privacy is essential if these fish are to be persuaded to spawn successfully; they will not do so in an open tank. As many as 500 eggs may be laid and once the fry are free-swimming, they will require large amounts of infusoria followed by brine shrimp *nauplii*.

In contrast to most *Cichlasoma* species, festive cichlids are relatively peaceful, especially outside the spawning period, but they must not be housed with neon tetras (*Paracheirodon innesi*) in particular, because these fish are likely to fall prey to them. Other smaller companions may also be inadvisable, but angelfish (*Pterophyllum* species) should prove to be suitable tank mates. Livefood needs to figure prominently in the diet of festive cichlids, but they will also eat some vegetable matter.

6in
15cm

Severum *(Heros severus)*

Another species which was formerly included with the *Cichlasoma* cichlids, the severum originates from northern South America. The presence of a vertical strip close to the caudal fin is the reason that this fish is also known as the banded cichlid. Young severums can be recognized by a series of such bands, which fade as the fish grow older. Sexing of mature individuals is possible, with males showing characteristic enlargement of the dorsal and anal fins as well as reddish-brown markings on the head.

8in
20cm

Lack of compatibility can be a problem when attempting to breed these cichlids and conditioning with livefood is also vital for successful spawning. They feed mainly on livefood, often displaying a preference for earthworms, while showing little, if any, interest in flake food. A varied diet should ensure a large brood, with as many as 1000 eggs being produced at a single spawning. Their subsequent development and the care of the fry follows the typical *Cichlasoma* pattern, although the severum tends not to disturb the substrate of the aquarium.

Convict Cichlid *(Heros nigrofasciatum)*

The striped appearance of these fish, with their grey background coloration, is reminiscent of prison uniform, which is why they acquired their unusual name. They may also be described as zebra cichlids. Their distribution extends from Guatemala southwards as far as Panama. These cichlids make an excellent introduction to this group of fish.

Convict cichlids will eat a wide range of foods, with less emphasis in their diet being placed on livefood. Green food is important and they will take a wide range of formulated fish foods, including food sticks and flake, although for conditioning purposes livefood such as bloodworms remain significant.

The longer fins of male convict cichlids can again serve to distinguish them from females. They are also less colourful overall, lacking the yellowish-orange suffusion seen on the female's underparts. It is not unknown for older males to develop a nuchal hump on the head.

These cichlids are definitely not suitable for a community aquarium since they are highly aggressive, especially as the time for spawning approaches. Plants should not be

6in
15cm

incorporated into their aquarium either, because these are likely to be excavated in due course. A gravel base, some rockwork and a clay flowerpot for spawning purposes, with floating plants on the surface, will suffice. Not all pairs will seek the seclusion of the flowerpot for breeding purposes however, preferring to spawn instead on a piece of slate in the open. Rearing presents no particular problems but not all pairs prove to be diligent parents, sometimes neglecting their brood at an early stage. This does not mean that the young fish will be lost, but it will be safer to rear them separately.

Jaguar Cichlid *(Heros managuense)*

The black spotted markings of these cichlids are responsible for their common name, although they are also sometimes described as Managua cichlids because of one of the lakes in which they occur in Nicaragua. Males tend to be more brightly coloured than females, and have more elaborate dorsal and anal fins.

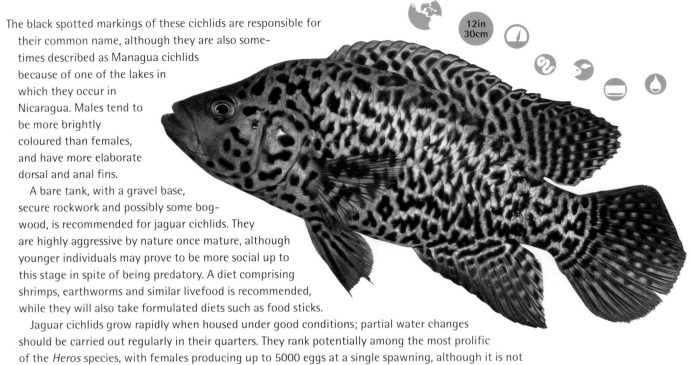

A bare tank, with a gravel base, secure rockwork and possibly some bogwood, is recommended for jaguar cichlids. They are highly aggressive by nature once mature, although younger individuals may prove to be more social up to this stage in spite of being predatory. A diet comprising shrimps, earthworms and similar livefood is recommended, while they will also take formulated diets such as food sticks.

Jaguar cichlids grow rapidly when housed under good conditions; partial water changes should be carried out regularly in their quarters. They rank potentially among the most prolific of the *Heros* species, with females producing up to 5000 eggs at a single spawning, although it is not easy to persuade them to breed in the first instance. Spawning is more likely to be successful in a suitable pond rather than aquarium surroundings.

Angelfish *(Pterophyllum scalare)*

These tall yet narrow fish are found in reedy stretches of water in the Amazon basin, where their shape allows them to weave and swim easily through the dense vegetation. Few fish look more elegant and angelfish are exceedingly popular among fishkeepers. Since first being kept in Europe back in 1909, they have been widely bred and a number of distinctive varieties now exist.

In some instances, the characteristic dark vertical bands of these fish have been lost, as in the case of the platinum form, and their coloration has altered, as in the golden variety sometimes described as the butterball. Changes to the banding have given rise to the marbled angelfish, with fin length being modified in the veil-tail form.

A well-planted tank with tough, upright plants such as *Sagittaria* is recommended for angelfish. Livefood is highly significant in their diet, although they should also be provided with some green food. They may also eat flake food sprinkled on the surface. Young angelfish will live in shoals but they will then start to pair off as they grow bigger. The depth of the tank is important for these fish, in view of their height, and should be 18in (45cm) or more for adult angelfish. Breeding details are identical to those of the deep angelfish (see below).

Deep Angelfish *(Pterophyllum altum)*

This species is also sometimes called the long-finned angelfish as the fins are particularly elongated. There is also a distinctive notch on the head above the eyes. It is less commonly available than the angelfish itself, but needs similar care. Deep angelfish inhabit the reedbeds of the Orinoco river and its tributaries.

It is impossible to sex these cichlids visually outside the breeding season, at which point females will swell with their spawn. Livefood is a very important conditioning food. The eggs are deposited on plants or slate and up to 1000 may be produced as the result of a single spawning.

The adult fish are attentive, fanning their eggs, removing any contaminated with fungus and even helping the fry to hatch. After hatching the fry dangle from a leaf, hanging off a thread produced from their head. Finally the fry are transferred to a hollow in the substrate. Their parents will guard them for a time even once they are swimming freely around the aquarium. Rotifers should be provided as an initial food.

Although it is often recommended to keep young angelfish in a community aquarium, their long trailing fins, especially those of this species, can make an irresistible target for smaller, nimble companions such as barbs, and this could lead to fungal infections developing. Furthermore, the rate of growth of angelfish is such that they will soon have outstripped the other fish in size and may well need a larger and deeper aquarium. Watch for signs of white spot when purchasing angelfish.

5in
12.5cm

Discus *(Symphysodon discus)*

Increasing numbers of aquarists have fallen under the charm of this cichlid in recent years and a wide range of colour varieties are now in existence. The wild forms of the discus actually appear to be quite drab in comparison. They have acquired a reputation for being rather delicate fish, but this dates back to the time before their requirements were fully understood.

If their needs in terms of water chemistry can be accommodated, then discus can be kept and bred without undue difficulty. They should ideally be accommodated in tanks only with others of their kind. Discus will live in shoals, but once a pair bond is obvious, the fish concerned should be separated from the other fish for spawning purposes. Unfortunately, there is no easy way of sexing them.

Discus require a diet of small livefood and can be persuaded to eat freeze-dried or other prepared foods of this type. The pair clean the chosen surface for the eggs, which may be a broad leaf or rockwork. About 200 or more eggs may be laid and the adult discus may eat them soon afterwards. Although disappointing, this is quite common behaviour in young pairs breeding for the first time and they are very likely to breed without any further problems when they spawn again, especially if left undisturbed.

Around 2 days after egg laying, the adult fish will help to free the young from the egg cases and attach them to aquatic plants. At 5 days old, the fry will be swimming and remain close to their parents, feeding on skin secretions on the sides of their body. At this stage, the young discus are elongated in shape. They gradually start to assume their characteristic disc-like appearance from the age of 3 months old. It will take a further 6 months however, for their coloration to develop fully.

8in
20cm

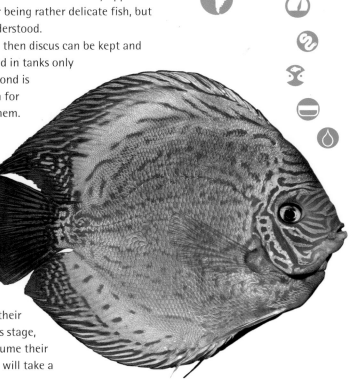

Orange Chromide *(Etroplus maculatus)*

These Asiatic cichlids are found in parts of western India and Sri Lanka, where they inhabit both fresh and brackish stretches of water. The addition of a little marine salt to their aquarium water not only helps to protect them from fungus, but also appears to emphasize their stunning coloration. Their body is covered with red dots, while black blotches are usually apparent on their flanks. Sexing can be problematical, although males tend to be more brightly coloured and have a red border to their fins, especially during the spawning period.

Orange chromides will eat mainly livefood and may take prepared foodstuffs on occasions as well. A well-planted tank with various hiding places is ideal but plastic plants may be the best option in view of the slightly salty nature of the water. Bogwood can also be useful and the fish may prefer to spawn here rather than on rocks.

A pair usually prove to be diligent parents and remain with their eggs, which may number up to 300 in total. They then watch over the fry when they hatch, keeping them in pits. Infusoria, followed by brine shrimp *nauplii*, can be used for rearing purposes, although it has been suggested that the fry also feed on their parents' flanks, like young discus.

3in
7.5cm

Jewel Cichlid *(Hemichromis bimaculatus)*

Found in parts of west Africa these colourful cichlids vary in colour, usually becoming orangish-red at spawning time. Some jewel cichlids remain permanently reddish however, rather than changing colour at the start of the spawning period. In other cases, these fish become yellowish, with small bluish dots on their flanks, for the remainder of the year. There is a black spot edged with yellow just above the pectoral fin on each side of the body and a similar marking may be evident at the base of the caudal fin, with another black area on the flank; these dark markings may be paler in females.

Jewel cichlids are really fish for the specialist, because a pair will need to be accommodated on their own. They can be highly aggressive tank wreckers and the male may even attack his prospective mate, with fatal consequences.

Compatibility is vital for successful breeding. Rockwork and a flowerpot should be provided, to offer a choice of spawning sites. Up to 500 eggs will be laid, with the young being moved at first to spawning pits. Infusoria or a commercial substitute should be used initially for rearing purposes. The small fry will then grow quite rapidly and may be mature when just 3in (7.5cm) long.

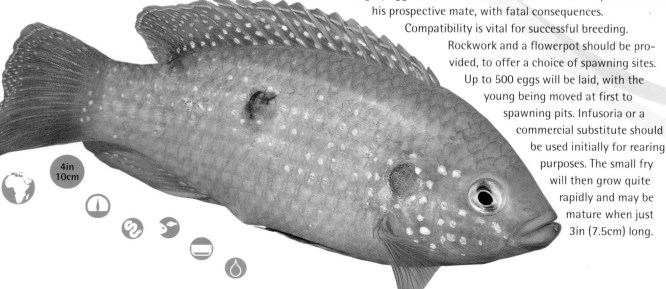

4in
10cm

Ahl's Haplochromis *(Haplochromis ahli)*

This is one of the many cichlids found in Lake Malawi in East Africa, where there are more than 100 recognized *Haplochromis* species alone. It is found in the open waters of the lake and is an active swimmer. The taxonomy of these fish is difficult, with this particular species being regarded as the same as *Cyrotara jacksoni* and sometimes classified accordingly.

Ahl's haplochromis is one of the most colourful lake cichlids, but it will take a year for males to acquire their deep, rich blue coloration. It may be better to start off with younger fish, especially since this tends to be one of the more costly species and you could otherwise end up pur-chasing an old male. There is also possibly less risk of incom-patibility during spawning if the fish have been reared together.

Males are highly aggressive towards other blue-coloured cichlids and may also harass females at the start of the breeding period–plenty of cover is important in their quarters. There may be as many as 100 eggs, but the fry will often grow at different rates with the larger young cannibalizing their siblings. This can result in an abnormally high proportion of male fish among surviving members of the brood, as they tend to grow faster.

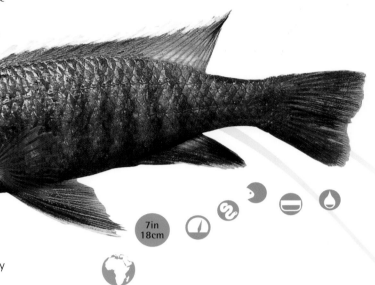

7in
18cm

Peacock Cichlid *(Aulonacara nyassae)*

These cichlids occur in rocky areas of Lake Malawi. They, like other Rift Valley cichlids, have specific water requirements and special salt mixes should be stirred and dissolved into the aquarium water to replicate their natural habitat as closely as possible. There is considerable variation in their coloration and markings, which has led to great confusion about the number of distinct species which exist. As a general guide, peacock cichlids are often bluish, with darker markings, and males tend to be more vibrantly coloured than females. This does vary however, because in an aquarium where there is more than one male, only the dominant individual will be brightly coloured with the other males resembling females in appearance.

Livefood such as bloodworm and *Daphnia* should feature prominently in the diet of these fish, along with a high-protein prepared food, as in the case of the previous species. It is a good idea, especially if you live in a soft water area, to use alkaline materials such as coral gravel (sold by aquatic shops) as the substrate. This should help to prevent the water from becoming acidic, which will not be tolerated well by this group of fish. Regular pH testing of their water is especially vital.

6in
15cm

Malawi Golden Cichlid *(Melanochromis auratus)*

Found in the shallows around the rocky shores of Lake Malawi, this cichlid can be sexed without difficulty. While the mature male is blackish, with a light stripe running down each side of its body, the female shows the characteristic golden markings on her flanks. These areas are separated by a black line bordered by white, with an upper black bar also apparent.

A single male should be housed in a 'species only' tank, in the company of several females. Malawi golden cichlids will not disturb vegetation in their quarters by burrowing into the substrate, although they tend to be herbivorous by nature and should be fed accordingly.

These fish are mouth-brooders. This means that the young fry hatch and develop in the mouth of their mother, who does not feed through this period. Even once the fry are free-swimming, they may return here if danger threatens. Up to 30 eggs may result from a single spawning and the female will retain a protective interest in her fry for as long as a week after they first emerge from her mouth.

Chipokae *(Melanochromis chipokae)*

Some cichlids in the Rift Valley lakes appear to have a very limited distribution here, for reasons which are not clearly understood. The chipokae–which is only known from the Chidunga Rocks, a rocky area in the south-west corner of Lake Malawi–is a member of this group.

It is an attractive fish with a bluish-black body offset against lighter blue areas on the upper parts and around the borders of the lower fins. White egg spots are apparent on the male's anal fin. Females and immatures are dull yellow with black markings in the form of two stripes encircling the body.

Their aquarium should be decorated with plenty of rocks to mimic their natural habitat. It needs to be large because these cichlids are aggressive by nature, both to individuals of their own species and other cichlids. They should only be housed with bigger fish from this part of the world, which will not be intimidated by them.

The chipokae tends to be a relatively predatory species in its feeding habits as well, with livefood featuring prominently in its diet. This species is mouth-brooding and the fry can be reared on similar food as recommended for *Pseudotropheus* species (see page 74). It may be better to allow the female to produce her offspring in a tank on her own.

Lemon Cichlid *(Lamprotogus leleupi)*

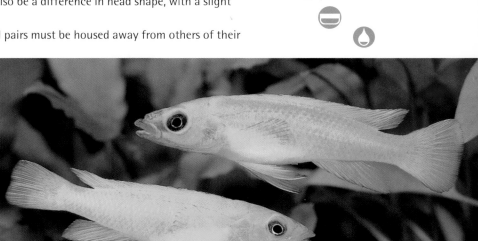

One of the most beautiful of all the cichlids this species originates from Lake Tanganyika, another of the huge expanses of water found in the Rift Valley of East Africa. The lemon cichlid is a stunning shade of yellow, with a trace of dark markings often apparent on the dorsal and other fins. Some subspecies are of a naturally richer shade of yellow than others, bordering almost on orange in some cases. This variation in coloration is not a means of distinguishing the sexes, but males do have longer pelvic fins than females. There may also be a difference in head shape, with a slight swelling here in the case of the male.

Lemon cichlids are monogamous by nature and pairs must be housed away from others of their kind. They will also prey on smaller fish sharing their quarters and it is important to remove older fry by the time they are about 6 weeks old. The adult cichlids are likely to spawn again at this stage and will resent the presence of their older offspring. Assorted livefoods should form the basis of the diet of these cichlids.

Plenty of retreats are necessary for lemon cichlids, so that they have a secluded area where they can spawn. A flowerpot may be used for this purpose and as many as 200 eggs can be laid at a single spawning. Both adults care for the fry, which should be offered infusoria at first. The young are likely to be mature by the age of 18 months.

Brichard's Lamprotogus *(Lamprotogus brichardii)*

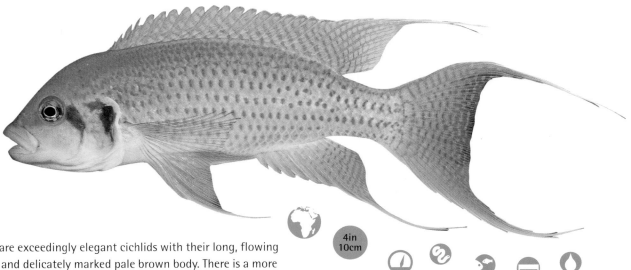

These are exceedingly elegant cichlids with their long, flowing fins and delicately marked pale brown body. There is a more prominent yellow area behind the eyes, while the fins all have bluish-white edges. A white form of this fish is also available on occasions. Females tend to be slightly smaller in size than males and the shape of their fins, particularly the caudal and dorsal, is less pronounced.

Although these cichlids live in shoals outside the breeding period, they do become territorial when spawning. The best means therefore of starting out with them is to acquire a group of young fish, which will ultimately form pairs; in a suitably large aquarium, they may even be persuaded to spawn communally without problems. Females of this species can produce as many as 200 eggs, although spawnings are generally smaller.

Livefood is an essential part of their diet, although these cichlids will also feed on flake and similar foods. The tank must include rockwork and retreats such as artificial caves for spawning purposes. The female will guard the fry. If she spawns again with her older brood still in the aquarium, they are also likely to assist her in protecting the newly hatched fry.

Tropheops *(Pseudotropheops tropheops)*

This cichlid is one of the Mbuna group, so called by the people who live around the western shores of Lake Malawi. This name means 'rockfish' and describes the habitat which these cichlids inhabit, although some may be found in sandy or reedy areas. The classification of these fish is complex and controversial, to the extent that there is likely to be more than one species currently represented under this name.

In all cases however, females vary from bright yellow to beige in colour, with young fish of both sexes being similarly coloured. Mature males are noticeably darker, ranging from brownish to grey, with a metallic bluish suffusion evident, especially on the sides of their body. These fish originate from the southern end of the lake.

6in
15cm

Tropheops cichlids have proved to be less aggressive than some of the other species that are found in the Rift Valley lakes, but males should be kept apart and housed separately with two or three females. Rockwork and a few tough plants should be used to decorate the aquarium. These cichlids will eat flake food, as well as greenstuff and livefood.

Females are mouth-brooders, with the fry emerging for the first time about 3 weeks after spawning. The young cichlids will be guarded by the females for a brief period while they start to feed on tiny livefood and powdered flake.

Zebra Malawi Cichlid *(Pseudotropheus zebra)*

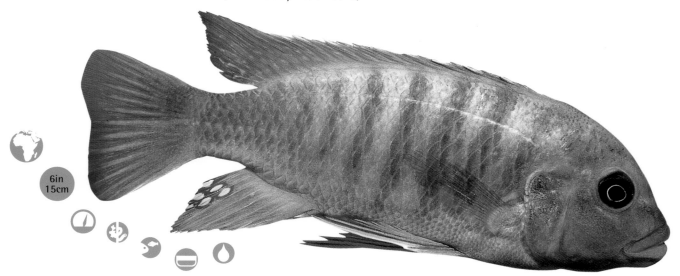

6in
15cm

Like a number of other cichlids from Lake Malawi these fish occur naturally in more than one colour form, which fuels the arguments as to whether they should be considered as a separate species. The majority of zebra Malawi cichlids are light blue, with dark blue stripes and a more pronounced dark blue area on their heads. There is also an orange morph, which has black blotches randomly distributed across its body. This population appears to consist almost entirely of female fish.

These cichlids are distributed right along the west coast of the lake. Here they appear to browse mainly on algae but aquarium specimens will eat a wide range of foods, especially those high in fibre such as spirulina.

In a large aquarium, zebra Malawi cichlids will generally agree well with other relatively non-aggressive species that naturally share their habitat. They are active fish, and groups comprising one male and several females should be selected for breeding purposes. Rockwork should be used to create natural areas of territory. Females may produce up to 60 eggs, which may take nearly 3 weeks to develop, and the female alone watches over her offspring once they leave her mouth.

Slender Mbuna *(Pseudotropheus elongatus)*

These cichlids show quite dramatic colour changes, depending in part on their environment. They are basically greyish-black with blue vertical stripes running down each side of their body. Slender mbunas rank among the more aggressive members of the genus and tend to be seen rather less often today than in the past, possibly for this reason. Sexing is reasonably straight-forward, with the so-called yellow egg patches on the anal fin of the male fish being brighter in coloration.

Care and breeding requirements are similar to that of other *Pseudotropheus* species. It is particularly important to keep a group of females with a male, to reduce the risk of aggression. Females will lay 20 or so eggs on rockwork, before taking them into their mouth where fertilization occurs. There is again no lasting pair bond and the female will look after the fry on her own once they leave her mouth. The young cichlids are likely to continue to remain in their mother's territory for a period, even when they no longer retreat within her mouth.

Julie *(Julidochromis ornatus)*

The *Julidochromis* cichlids are confined to Lake Tanganyika. They have a relatively narrow body shape, emphasized by the two brown stripes running along the sides of their bodies through the eyes down to the caudal fin. A further chocolate area highlights the base of the dorsal fin, with the remainder of the body being yellowish.

This is one of the more colourful members of the genus. Unfortunately, sexing is very difficult with differences in coloration being of no value. Those from the northern part of the lake are far more colourful than others occurring in the south, where the yellow areas are replaced by ivory.

Julies feed both on livefood and prepared foods such as flake and they will not damage plants. Rockwork is vital for breeding pur-poses, because these cichlids belong to the cave spawning group. They are monoga-mous, and pairs need to be kept apart. The female will typically produce up to 50 eggs and the fry will usually remain close to the concealed area of rockwork where they hatched, even after they have been free-swimming for a time.

Although females may only lay relatively small numbers of eggs, they may well spawn more frequently than other cichlids. Hatching typically takes about two and a half days, with the fry being free-swimming in a further 5 days. Small livefood and powdered flake food is suitable for rearing purposes.

Fuelleborn's Cichlid *(Labeotropheus fuelleborni)*

There have been 20 different forms of this particular cichlid described and more may still await
discovery in Lake Malawi where they occur. The
coloration of these fish therefore varies widely;
the most common variety is light blue with
darker markings, while females are of a more
greyish tone. In all cases, males tend to be
larger and display the so-called yellow egg
spots on their anal fin, while there is also an
orangish, mainly female variety marked with
black spots.

Although they tend to be vegetarian in their
feeding habits, these cichlids are aggressive and
males must be kept apart as they mature. They
start to gain their adult coloration by the time
they are about 2.5in (7cm) long. Even in large
tanks, males are likely to be pugnacious towards
related species showing similar coloration.

Rockwork is important as a means of provid-
ing retreats and territorial boundaries for females. Algal
growth on the rocks will also provide a source of nutrients for
these fish, although formulated foods and livefood will be
required as well.

One of the distinctive characteristics of these cichlids is their
low mouth, which enables them to browse on algae without
having to position themselves vertically in the water to do so.

  6in 15cm

Fuelleborn's cichlids reproduce by mouth-brooding, with no
lasting pair bond being established between the partners.
Details are similar to those of other cichlids displaying this
pattern of reproduction.

Green Lethrinops *(Lethrinops furcifer)*

There are at least four distinctive colour varieties of this cichlid from Lake Malawi. Sexing is possible, as
mature males are an attractive shade of blue while females are paler and lack any egg spots on their
anal fin. This is not an aggressive species and these cichlids can be kept communally, although only the
dominant male will assume full breeding colour. They are in fact at risk of being bullied by other smaller
cichlids so a species tank can be recommended for them.

Planting the aquarium for green lethrinops is futile, because any vegetation is likely to be uprooted. They will search for food by
digging the substrate and will also excavate pits for
breeding purposes. If rockwork is included in the
aquarium the male may carry sand in his
mouth, building a nest
on the top of the rock as
occurs in the wild.

Females lay about 20
eggs or so on average,
although more may some-
times be produced. The eggs
are picked up and carried in
the mouth, with the female
following the male closely to collect his sperm.
Fertilization occurs here and the young cichlids will emerge from their mother's mouth
about 3 weeks later. Brine shrimp *nauplii* can then be provided for rearing purposes. Males are slower to
mature than females, taking about 18 months. A relatively high degree of infertility may therefore be
noted in early broods from young green lethrinops which will be resolved in due course.

LABYRINTH FISH

The unusual name of these fish stems from the presence of a labyrinth organ, located in the head close to the gills, comprising a well-developed set of blood vessels to absorb oxygen. This enables these fish to breathe atmospheric air directly, which is an important adaptation for their survival because they normally inhabit poorly oxygenated stretches of muddy water. On occasions, some species, especially the climbing perches, may even venture on to land.

Labyrinth fish, also known as anabantids, originate from parts of Africa and Asia. They are sometimes called bubble nest builders, because male fish generally construct a nest for the eggs consisting of bubbles of saliva at the water's surface. Some males can be exceptionally aggressive, notably in the case of the Siamese fighting fish, and must be kept separate from each other. Equally, certain species can grow very large and will outgrow an aquarium rapidly.

Siamese Fighting Fish *(Betta splendens)*

The distribution of these popular aquarium fish is centred in Thailand and, even in the case of wild Siamese fighting fish, there can be considerable variation in their coloration. As domestication has taken place, so the fins of males have become more elaborate than those of the native form and their appearance has become more colourful. While the tendency is for shades of brown, dull red and blue to appear in wild fish, brilliant pure red and even yellow variants are now available in aquarium strains.

The males are highly aggressive by nature and will fight viciously, so there should never be more than one housed in an aquarium. They tend not to interfere with other occupants however, even those with similar coloration to themselves. Female Siamese fighting fish can be distinguished easily, by their much duller brownish coloration and short fins. Livefood, especially mosquito larvae, should feature prominently in the diet of these fish, while whiteworm is also valuable for conditioning.

A pair will need to be transferred to a separate tank for breeding. Here, the male will prepare the characteristic bubble nest on the surface of the water, using saliva to trap air and form the bubbles. The female will lay up to 500 eggs, which will be collected and carried to the nest by her partner. Each spawning embrace results in the release of 15 eggs or so, with the entire process taking about 2 hours.

The female can then be removed and the male will guard the eggs and the fry when they hatch around 2 days later. They

3in
7.5cm

will need a suitable fry food, or rotifers if these are available, having very small mouths at this stage. Regular small feeds through the day are essential, accompanied by careful water changes as the fry grow. The tank must be kept covered, to prevent chilling. Separate the male Siamese fighting fish once they are 3 months old.

Peaceful Betta *(Betta imbellis)*

As its name suggests, this fish is far less aggressive than Siamese fighting fish. Even when spawning, male peaceful bettas are not as tyrannical. Sexing presents no difficulties, since females are basically brown in colour with both sexes darkening in colour as the time for spawning approaches. It is even possible to house several pairs of these bettas together, if they are all introduced to the aquarium at the same time. They require a densely planted tank, with other decor such as bogwood being included. Floating plants also help to replicate the slow flowing stretches of water where these bettas naturally occur.

Livefood will again serve to trigger spawning activity. It is important to move the adult bettas however, because the delicate bubble nest constructed by the male will be destroyed if, for example, there is a power filter creating strong currents in the aquarium. The female only lays a relatively small number of eggs, in bursts, and is essentially immobile during this stage. Once they hatch, after a period of 6 days, the fry can be reared quite easily on suitably small food.

The peaceful betta is a comparatively recent introduction to the aquatic scene, first being kept in 1970. It is still not perhaps as well known among aquarists as it deserves to be, especially in view of its attractive appearance and amenable nature.

2in
5cm

Paradise Fish *(Macropodus opercularis)*

This has proved to be a very hardy tropical fish, quite capable of surviving at temperatures down to 50°F (10°C). It may have been first kept outside its native habitat during the 1600s, with fish of similar appearance being recorded in London by the famous diarist Samuel Pepys.

4in
10cm

Male paradise fish can be distinguished by their brighter coloration and longer fins. Alternating bluish and orange stripes run down the sides of their bodies. There is a less well-known subspecies found in South China which is significantly darker in coloration; it is sometimes classified as a distinct species–*M. concolo* –with males in this case being almost black.

Male paradise fish will prove to be disruptive in an aquarium if housed with other similar species and need to be kept apart from each other. The male is often very determined when courting and the planting scheme should provide retreats for the female or she may lose condition. The aquarium must also be covered, since these fish can jump well.

Breeding can usually be stimulated by transferring the fish to a tank where the water level is lowered, while the temperature is gradually raised by several degrees to 82°F (28°C). Increasing the livefood content of their diet also helps. A typical bubble nest is constructed, often around a leaf, and as many as 500 eggs may be produced by the female. The resulting fry will be free-swimming about 4 days later. Suitably small food such as infusoria will be required in quantity at this stage.

Spike-tailed Paradise Fish *(Macropodus cupanus)*

The coloration of these anabantids is highly variable, tending to be primarily brownish on the
body. The anal fin is marked with red, while the
dorsal and caudal fins are bluish. During the
spawning period males can be easily distinguished by their red coloration while females
assume a blackish body coloration. Spike-tailed
paradise fish can be easily identified by the
presence of obvious elongations trailing at the
rear of the caudal fin, although these may be lost
on occasions if the water quality is poor or if the
fins are nipped by other fish.

Feeding presents no difficulties as they will eat
prepared foods such as flake, although livefood is
preferred. Good lighting is also helpful because it
promotes the growth of algae, which will
supplement the diet of these fish. A relatively
shallow aquarium is recommended, especially for
breeding purposes, with bogwood included.
Bogwood or rockwork can provide a point of
attachment for the bubble nest; a broad leaf will
also suffice, with the bubble nest being submerged
in this case. Rearing of the fry should be similar to
that of related species. The adult fish will not usually
molest their offspring.

  3in 7.5cm

Spotted Climbing Perch *(Ctenopoma acutirostre)*

Climbing perches are so called because they can move on land,
using their pectoral fins to drag themselves along
and breathing via their
labyrinth organ. This
species comes from the
central African country of
Zaire. It is sometimes called
the leopard bushfish, because
of its markings. It may be possible
to sex these fish on the basis that
males are more heavily spotted and
have spinous areas on their bodies.

Climbing perches have rather predatory natures
and livefood, including small earthworms for larger
individuals, should form the basis of their diet. They
will take freeze-dried foods. These fish are rather
inactive by nature and they tend to take prey by
ambushing rather than by active hunting.

Spotted climbing perches have been bred in aquarium
surroundings, and appear to have a long reproductive life–pairs
over 10 years old have spawned successfully. The male builds a
bubble nest and the young hatch within 2 days. They can be
reared in a similar way to other anabantids.

 6in 15cm

Pearl Gourami *(Trichogaster leerii)*

The white markings on the flanks of these fish are bright, displaying the lustre of pearls. This species is also sometimes described as the lace gourami, because of its intricate patterning. Sexing is possible once these gouramis are around 7 months old and reach a size of about 3in (7.5cm) in length. This is the stage at which the characteristic red coloration of males starts to become apparent on their underparts. Their dorsal and anal fins also develop rays and, for this reason, it is usually unwise to house them with potential fin-nipping companions, particularly barbs.

Pearl gouramis benefit from being kept in a relatively shallow aquarium, about 4in (10cm) deep, as the time for spawning approaches. It needs to be comparatively large however, in view of the fact that as many as 1000 or more fry may result. Some plants can be grouped within the tank, while floating plants on the surface are important as these are likely to be used as an anchor point for the bubble nest. As with other breeding anabantids, care needs to be taken with the filtration system in the spawning tank to ensure that it will not destroy the nest. After mating, the male will concentrate on looking after the eggs. Once the fry are free-swimming, after 3 days or so, he can be transferred back to the main aquarium. These fish may live for around 8 years.

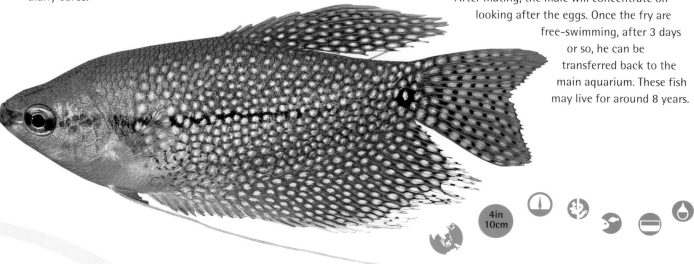

4in
10cm

Three-spot Gourami *(Trichogaster trichopterus)*

This species is also known as the blue gourami because of its distinctive natural coloration, although various colour variants, most notably a golden form, have been developed as the result of domestication. The pointed dorsal fin of the mature male serves to distinguish the sexes in any event, irrespective of their coloration.

These gouramis are very easy to care for, although they will not prove to be active tank occupants. Any companions therefore need to be chosen with care to ensure they will not persecute the gouramis, which is likely to result in a loss of colour. Males must be kept separate because they can be aggressive towards each other.

Reasonably large spawning tanks are also important as some males will prove aggressive and females must have space and cover in the form of plants so they can retreat when necessary. The male three-spot gourami will construct a large bubble nest among floating plants. The nest can have a diameter of 10in (25cm), which is another reason for housing the fish in a good sized aquarium at this stage. Relatively shallow water is again preferable, with the female being removed after spawning. As many as 1000 fry may result, although the colour varieties tend to produce smaller broods.

4in
10cm

Moonlight Gourami *(Trichogaster microlepis)*

These silvery gouramis have very small scales which serve
to emphasize their shiny appearance. The
thread-like pelvic fins provide an easy
means of distinguishing the
sexes, being yellowish in the
case of females and a more
definite shade of red in male
fish. Their dorsal fin is also more
elongated, as in related species.

The distribution of the moonlight
gourami is centred in Thailand. Their feeding
and general care present no particular problems.
These fish will eat a variety of foods, including algae, flake
food and freeze-dried items. Barbs should be avoided as
companions in a mixed collection because they may damage
their fins, but other anabantids or even some characins will be
suitable. Again, it is important to make sure that the water is
changed every 2 weeks or so.

The bubble nest of the moonlight gourami may extend
nearly 1in (2.5cm) above the surface of the water. The male
will use pieces of plant matter in the nest to provide support
for the nest, damaging *Myriophyllum* and similar narrow-
leaved plants in the tank for this purpose. Breeding and rearing
details do not otherwise differ significantly from those of
related species of anabantids.

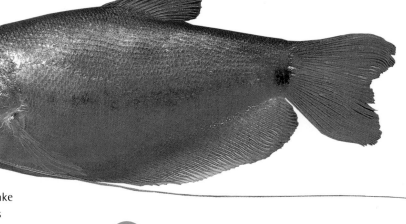

Chocolate Gourami *(Sphaerichthys osphromenoides)*

These gouramis have proved to be one of the more difficult
species to maintain and breed successfully in aquarium surroundings. The presence of a yellow border on the dorsal and
anal fins signifies a male. Chocolate gouramis live in ditches
and other similar slow flowing areas of water where there is
dense vegetative cover. Most significantly however, the water
itself has a very low mineral content and is relatively warm.

The use of a peat extract is important, and regular water
changes every fortnight or so are essential to the wellbeing of
these fish. Unlike many other anabantids, the chocolate
gourami is not a bubble nest builder. Instead, the female will
lay around 80 eggs, which are fertilized by the male. She then
collects them in her mouth, and retreats to a secluded part of
the aquarium.

The young fry are released from the female's mouth approximately 14–19 days later, by which stage they resemble adults
in coloration. Brine shrimp *nauplii* can be used in this instance
as a rearing food and the fry grow fast, more than doubling
their size to over 0.5in (1.25cm) in just
3 weeks. Maintain the water quality by
frequent partial changes. The female
chocolate gourami will show no maternal
instincts once the fry have left her mouth.

Kissing Gourami *(Helostoma temmincki)*

Although the wild form of this fish is silvery-grey in colour, the rose-pink domesticated variety is now more commonly available. Sexing by visual means is almost totally impossible outside the breeding period, when the female swells with eggs. These gouramis can grow to a relatively large size and are bred commercially, not only for the aquarium trade, but also as a source of food in various parts of southern Asia.

Kissing gouramis have thick lips which serve to help them browse on algae. They can be useful for this purpose in the aquarium but, unfortunately, they will also destroy vegetation, to the point that plastic plants may be essential. It may be possible to deter such damage to some extent by providing greenstuff such as lettuce as part of their regular diet.

Adding lettuce leaves on the surface of the spawning tank is also often recommended to encourage the development of infusoria, which will nourish the fry when they hatch. Kissing gouramis do not construct a proper bubble nest, although males may produce a series of bubbles on occasions. After spawning, the adult fish should be removed; the eggs will then float on the surface and will hatch after a period of approximately 4 days. The strange way in which kissing gouramis touch lips is not part of the spawning process–instead, it probably allows territorial disputes to be amicably resolved without the need for more overt displays of aggression.

Gourami *(Osphronemus goramy)*

This gourami can potentially outgrow all but the largest aquaria and it is rarely kept as a result, although young stock may sometimes be available. The gourami is extensively farmed in Asia for food. Young of this species, up to about 6in (15cm) in length, differ significantly in appearance from adults. Their bronzy-greyish body is transversed by broad dark bars while the head is distinctly pointed, so they can be confused at this stage with the chocolate gourami (see page 81). As these fish grow larger however, the markings fade, and their lips thicken considerably. There is also a whitish domesticated form of this gourami.

Their growth rate is very fast, with young fish in good conditions reaching 10in (25cm) long in a year from hatching. They mature even more rapidly however, sometimes breeding at just 6 months of age.

Vegetation in the tank will be stripped to assemble their ball-shaped nest, which is actually likely to be anchored among plants. Bubbles form little part in its construction, although it may prove to be substantial in size. The male, recognizable by his elongated dorsal and anal fins, will guard the nest until the fry are ready to leave, which is likely to take 2–3 weeks. They should then be reared separately, because they could fall victim to their larger relative.

Croaking Gourami *(Trichopsis vittatus)*

Members of this genus tend to have a narrower body shape than other gouramis. The distribution of the croaking gourami extends from mainland Asia, where it is found in Vietnam and Thailand, south to the Sunda Islands. There is considerable variation in appearance through their wide range. As a guide males tend to be more colourful, but this is not an entirely reliable means of distinguishing the sexes. *Trichopsis vittatus* is the largest of three species of croaking gourami, which do actually make a croaking sound, especially during the spawning period.

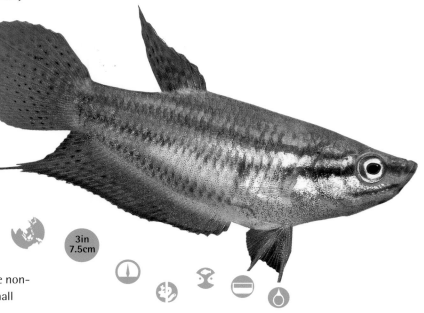

Dense planting in their aquarium is recommended, with floating plants providing additional cover for them. Croaking gouramis can be housed with suitable non-aggressive companions of similar size. A variety of small foodstuffs, including livefood, should be supplied.

Breeding is not especially easy. The water level should not exceed 4in (10cm), while the temperature should be raised to 86°F (30°C). The bubble nest will be built by the male at the water's surface, or may be concealed under plants there.

Leaving the pair together after spawning can encourage more devoted parental care by the male. An average spawning will consist of about 200 eggs, with the fry swimming freely by 4 days old. They can be reared at first on brine shrimp *nauplii*.

Dwarf Gourami *(Colisa lalia)*

Males of this species are particularly colourful, with brilliant blue markings superimposed on an orangish background. In contrast, females are far more silvery. The origins of the dwarf gourami lie in the north-east of India and the adjoining area of Bangladesh.

Quiet and sometimes rather shy by nature, these gouramis require similar companions. There must be plenty of vegetation in their aquarium and water quality is important, with regular partial changes being essential to their wellbeing.

Only after spawning is completed is the male dwarf gourami likely to become aggressive towards his mate, and she should be removed from the spawning tank at this stage. He builds a bubble nest, usually incorporating floating plants, which may extend nearly 1in (2.5cm) above the surface of the water.

Development of the fry is reasonably rapid, since they are free-swimming in just two and a half days. As many as 600 fry can result from a single spawning. Infusoria can be used initially for rearing purposes, followed by larger items including brine shrimp *nauplii*. The tank must be kept covered to maintain the air temperature, as for other young anabantids.

Thick-lipped Gourami *(Colisa labiosa)*

The brighter coloration of the male thick-lipped gourami provides a relatively simple means of distinguishing the sexes. The shape of the dorsal fin also offers another means of separation, since that of females is rounded whereas that of males is pointed. These gouramis originate from the vicinity of northern India, Bangladesh and Myanmar (formerly Burma).

The lips of these fish are relatively prominent, as their name suggests. These may help them to graze effectively on algae, which features in their diet along with other greenstuff. They will eat a range of formulated foods, including both pellets and flake.

A typical breeding set-up, as recommended for related species, should lead to successful spawning. Care needs to be taken not to damage the rather fragile bubble nest however, which is very large and will extend over much of the surface of the tank. The male continues to expand the nest after egg laying has occurred, having turned much darker in colour at the start of the spawning period.

A female is likely to produce around 500 eggs, which will float up into the nest or will be carried there by the male. Hatching takes place after a day, with the young being free-swimming by 3 days old. They require infusoria at first, followed by brine shrimp *nauplii* from the age of 10 days onwards.

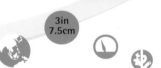

3in
7.5cm

Giant Gourami *(Colisa fasciata)*

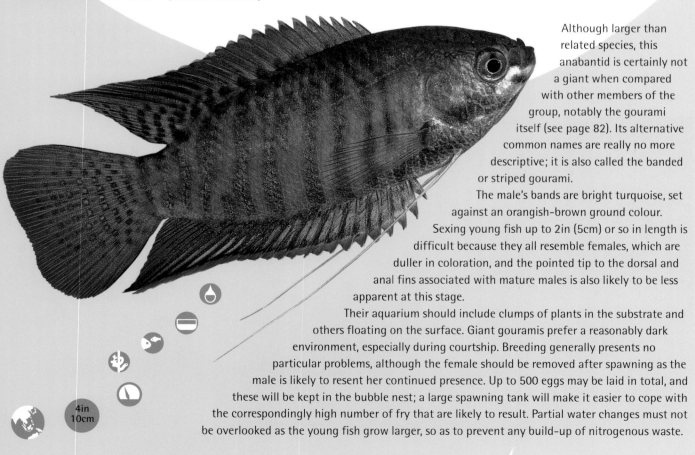

Although larger than related species, this anabantid is certainly not a giant when compared with other members of the group, notably the gourami itself (see page 82). Its alternative common names are really no more descriptive; it is also called the banded or striped gourami.

The male's bands are bright turquoise, set against an orangish-brown ground colour. Sexing young fish up to 2in (5cm) or so in length is difficult because they all resemble females, which are duller in coloration, and the pointed tip to the dorsal and anal fins associated with mature males is also likely to be less apparent at this stage.

Their aquarium should include clumps of plants in the substrate and others floating on the surface. Giant gouramis prefer a reasonably dark environment, especially during courtship. Breeding generally presents no particular problems, although the female should be removed after spawning as the male is likely to resent her continued presence. Up to 500 eggs may be laid in total, and these will be kept in the bubble nest; a large spawning tank will make it easier to cope with the correspondingly high number of fry that are likely to result. Partial water changes must not be overlooked as the young fish grow larger, so as to prevent any build-up of nitrogenous waste.

4in
10cm

KILLIFISH

These fish, also known as the egg laying toothcarps, have a wide distribution. Representatives of the group are found in the extreme south-west of Europe, as well as Africa and Asia and parts of the Americas. The so called annual killifish have a fascinating breeding cycle. In the wild these fish effectively die out after each generation. Their lifestyle is closely linked with the seasons in their home-lands as they typically inhabit relatively shallow stretches of water which evaporate during the dry season, resulting in their death. Their eggs, however, which are laid and fertilized as the water level falls, will survive in the mud as it dries and can hatch up to two years later when the rains return. A practical ben-efit for the aquarist is that this means that it can be easy to obtain stock from fellow breeders elsewhere in the country, since you may simply be able to purchase eggs by mail and then hatch them at home.

The requirements of these fish are fairly specialized. Their care and breeding presents no particular problems however, although insect food should feature prominently in their diet. Other killifish spawn in a more typical egg laying fashion among the vegetation in their aquarium.

Lyretail *(Aphyosemion australe)*

There are more than 60 species forming the genus *Aphyosemion* and the majority are represented in aquaria around the world. In spite of their rather specialist requirements, these killifish can be bred without too much difficulty.

The lyretail itself was introduced to the hobby back in 1913. Males are especially colourful, with bluish-green sides to their body and prominent red spots. The name of these killifish stems from the extended rays to the caudal fin, which create a lyre-tailed appearance. This species is also sometimes called the Cape Lopez lyretail, on the basis of the locality in West Africa where it was first obtained.

Dark surroundings, including a peat base to their aquarium and floating plants at the surface, are recommended. The peat will act as a natural disinfectant and will help to protect the killifish from bacterial infections. It is also usually recom-mended that some sea salt be added to the aquarium, creating a 5% solution.

Livefoods are favoured, but lyretails will also eat other foods including flake. In terms of breeding behaviour, the lyretail is one of the group of killifish which will spawn among plants rather than burying their eggs in the substrate. The eggs should be moved to a hatching tank, where the fry will hatch within 3 weeks. Water conditions in the hatching tank should not differ from those in the spawning tank.

3in
7.5cm

Steel-blue Aphyosemion *(Aphyosemion gardneri)*

Males of this species are predominantly blue with prominent red markings, although the upper part of the body is olive-green. Yellow edging to the fins is often apparent. Females, in contrast, are less colourful, with brownish dots extending down their flanks. The steel-blue aphyosemion originates from West Africa, where it is found in Nigeria, with a distribution extending to the Cameroons. A number of colour variations have been recorded through its range.

The steel-blue aphyosemion will thrive in a similar environment to that recommended above for the lyretail, but marine salt should not be added to the water in this case. Males can prove to be quite aggressive, both among themselves and towards intended mates. A relatively shallow spawning tank decorated with plants is required for spawning purposes.

Females tend to lay clusters of eggs every day, producing perhaps 400 or so over the course of a month. The eggs should be removed on a daily basis; this can be accomplished by washing the spawning medium in a hatching tank and then replacing it. Willow moss (*Fontinalis* species) spread out over the substrate is a favoured spawning plant for these fish. Hatching will again take about 3 weeks.

Striped Aphyosemion *(Aphyosemion striatum)*

Red lines rather than spots on the flanks help to distinguish males of this species. In contrast, females are a subdued shade of olive. Their housing should be similar to that of related species and salt can be added in this case. Even though the water level in the aquarium may be relatively low, the tank should still be covered to prevent any risk of these fish leaping out of their accommodation. Their diet should be based on livefood, with items such as mosquito larvae being especially favoured.

Aphyosemion killifish can be divided broadly into two groups on the basis of their breeding habits. One group, including this species, breed among vegetation. They inhabit what are normally permanent areas of water, even during the dry season. As a result, their eggs are sensitive to dessication and need to be kept in water. The second group, known as the annual killifish group, includes species that spawn on the substrate.

The striped aphyosemion is a relatively peaceful species and this simplifies the spawning process. Its eggs should be removed to a separate set-up on a daily basis, where hatching is likely to take just over a fortnight. Infusoria and then brine shrimp *nauplii* can be used for rearing purposes. In view of the protracted laying period, it is recommended that batches of small tanks are set up.

Red Lyretail *(Aphyosemion bivittatum)*

This particular killifish is also known as the two-striped aphyosemion, because of the characteristic two dark stripes running down each side of its body. Males are reddish-brown, with crimson spots which extend to the fins. Their dorsal, caudal and anal fins are extended, whereas those of females have a more rounded shape. There is considerable local variation in appearance through the range of this species however, and the subspecies described as *A. b. hollyi* displays predominantly blue coloration, with the result that it is sometimes known as the blue aphyosemion.

Spawning occurs among plants or an artificial substitute, which may offer a more hygienic option. A clean environment is important for this group of fish, both for their health and to ensure that a high percentage of their eggs hatch successfully in due course. Water from the spawning tank should be used in the hatching set-up. A single male can be accommodated with several females for breeding purposes.

Keeping the fish well fed during the protracted spawning period is important, but offer small amounts of food frequently as this will lessen the risk of food being left uneaten and polluting the water. Interestingly, not all the different varieties of this species will breed successfully with each other, confirming that there may be a case for dividing the existing species unit. It is important not to crossbreed, but to keep strains pure as far as possible. Genetic studies are being used to unravel the chromosomal patterns of these and other fish, and seem likely to have a great impact on classificatory arguments in the future.

Gularis *(Aphyosemion gulare)*

It is now thought that a number of different species are classified under this single heading. There can certainly be wide variations in appearance between individual gularis killifish in terms of coloration. These have tended to become more pronounced as aquarium strains have been developed. The yellow variety has a mainly yellowish-green body, becoming pale on the underparts, with purplish markings. Blue predominates in the case of the blue gularis, with vibrant red blotches on the sides of the body. Females in both cases are less brightly coloured.

These killifish tend to be more aggressive than other *Aphyosemion* species, and are best kept in small groups comprising one male and several females. In this case, a bowl should be placed on the floor of the spawning tank containing about 2in (5cm) of peat, or the entire floor area can be covered with peat. The eggs will be laid there and may be fanned into the substrate by the fin movements of the fish. After 3 weeks or so the adult fish should be transferred elsewhere and the water in the tank carefully removed, leaving just the peat base; this should remain slightly moist and must not dry out.

Between 1 and 3 months later, place the peat back in a tank and refill with soft water. The young fry should then begin to hatch over a period of time. Adding small amounts of powdered flake food seems to speed up this process. Rotifers and brine shrimp *nauplii* should be offered as the main part of the diet.

Walker's Aphyosemion *(Aphyosemion walkeri)*

Some killifish, like gularis, may breed both in plants and in the substrate. These fish occur in areas of water that may evaporate during the dry season and substrate spawning will ensure the species' survival in such habitats. Although the adult killifish die at this stage, their progeny hatch as the rains return and refill the water courses.

Walker's aphyosemion is a particularly attractive species. Males have elaborate dorsal, anal and caudal fins which are often mainly orange with crimson borders, while females are less colourful. The water temperature also influences their coloration–as it increases, they become paler–and shortens their life span. This group are sometimes called annual killifish because in the wild, where they live in temporary puddles, they would be unlikely to survive any longer than one year. In aquarium surroundings, their life expectancy can be extended, although they do not rank among the most long-lived of tropical fish.

If the eggs of Walker's aphyosemion are left in the water, they are likely to take about a month or so to hatch; if they are removed in peat, about 6 weeks should be allowed before the eggs are flooded with water again.

Blue Panchax *(Aplocheilus panchax)*

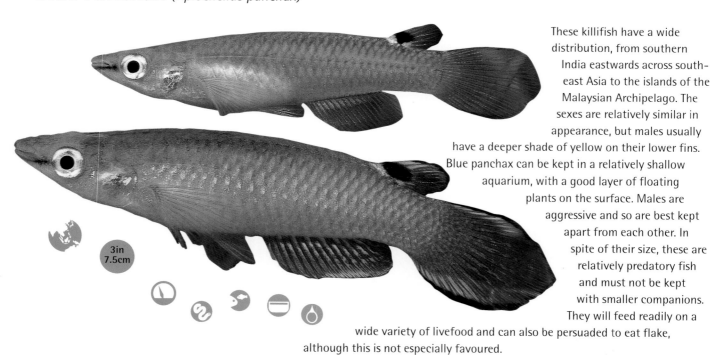

These killifish have a wide distribution, from southern India eastwards across south-east Asia to the islands of the Malaysian Archipelago. The sexes are relatively similar in appearance, but males usually have a deeper shade of yellow on their lower fins. Blue panchax can be kept in a relatively shallow aquarium, with a good layer of floating plants on the surface. Males are aggressive and so are best kept apart from each other. In spite of their size, these are relatively predatory fish and must not be kept with smaller companions. They will feed readily on a wide variety of livefood and can also be persuaded to eat flake, although this is not especially favoured.

Spawning is reasonably easy to accomplish, especially when the water is being filtered through peat. Fine-leaved plants will be used as a spawning medium. Egg laying is a relatively protracted affair, taking place over several weeks. The plants should be transferred to a rearing tank, where the fry can hatch unmolested by the adult fish. They will emerge after about 14 days and can be reared on a diet of rotifers and brine shrimp *nauplii*.

Green Panchax *(Aplocheilus blockii)*

This species is the smallest member of the genus and is sometimes known as the dwarf panchax as a result. It originates from southern India and Sri Lanka. Males are yellowish-green in colour, with some displaying red dots on their flanks, while females are of a paler shade and have more rounded fins.

The green panchax has a social nature in comparison with its larger relatives, both towards its fellows and other fish of similar size. Livefood must figure prominently in the diet of these killifish, with mosquito larvae proving to be a good conditioning food for breeding purposes.

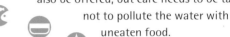

Green panchax spawn in vegetation, with moss or even an artificial substitute being provided for this purpose. Since spawning will occur over 2 weeks or so, it is better to have several small tanks set up for rearing purposes. Once the fry start to hatch, after about 14 days, infusoria and rotifers can be offered, followed by brine shrimp *nauplii*. Powdered flake food may also be offered, but care needs to be taken not to pollute the water with uneaten food.

Playfair's Panchax *(Pachypanchax playfairii)*

Found in East Africa and offshore islands including the Seychelles and Madagascar, this species is also known as the golden panchax. It is not, however, a very brightly coloured killifish; it is essentially yellowish-brown with orangish dots on its flanks. Golden-yellow coloration may be more apparent on the fins. Females are less brightly coloured than males and have an obvious black area at the base of the dorsal fin; males have a black border to their caudal fin.

The body surface of the male appears uneven as the scales here are raised, but this is not a sign of ill health. Some of these scales may be shed on occasions, typically during the spawning process.

Playfair's panchax is a predatory and aggressive killifish that will feed mainly on livefood which pass close by, lurking in wait among plants and ambushing its prey. Do not mix this panchax with smaller companions, which are liable to be eaten.

Dense planting should be a feature of a spawning tank for these fish, since this will help to protect their eggs from being

eaten. It must also be covered, to prevent the killifish from leaping out. Transfer the eggs to a hatching tank as they are laid. Spawning in this species takes place over about a week, during which time as many as 200 eggs may be produced. Hatching takes 12 days or so, with the young being reared on brine shrimp *nauplii*. Playfair's panchax may also be kept in brackish water, if it is carefully acclimatized to these conditions.

Entre Rio Pearlfish *(Cynolebias alexandri)*

Members of this genus are found in the southern part of South America, often in temporary pools of water. They are naturally short-lived, with a life expectancy of less than a year. Pearlfish are so called because of the characteristic white markings on the body and fins. They can be paired easily; males are more colourful than females, which are yellowish-brown and frequently have darker bands on the sides of their bodies. Males in breeding condition darken noticeably in colour. Both sexes have a blackish band encircling the eyes.

Cynolebias species should be kept in fairly dark aquaria, with peat as a substrate. Few plants can be included. Both livefood, such as whiteworm, and some flake food will be eaten. The water temperature should be kept relatively low, since higher temperatures appear to hasten their demise.

It is a good idea to keep the sexes apart prior to spawning, and then introduce a male and two females together. A soft substrate is needed so that the eggs can be directly deposited here. Subsequently, this will need to be dried out until it feels just damp. Several months later the peat can be tipped out into a tank; when the tank is refilled with soft water, the young pearlfish should start to hatch soon afterwards.

3in
7.5cm

Dwarf Argentine Pearlfish *(Cynolebias nigripennis)*

2in
5cm

There are again marked differences between the sexes in this case. Males are bluish-black, whereas females are grey and lack the iridescent spots present on the fins of males. These killifish should be kept in a similar way to the preceding species, with regular partial water changes being valuable.

Their breeding behaviour is also basically identical and their eggs will need to be stored in a similar fashion. The embryo are slower to develop than in the case of other annual killifish, such as the *Aphyosemion* species, and even when they all appear to have hatched it is often worthwhile drying out the substrate again, waiting a few more months, and repeating the process on several occasions. The eggs can remain viable for up to 3 years. Further fry are then likely to emerge at this stage.

This system of hatching has probably evolved to ensure that in the wild at least one group of these fry would have the opportunity to mature and breed before the pools of water evaporate. The young killifish grow rapidly, as might be expected. The characteristic differences between the sexes are apparent within 4 days, and by 2 months old these fish are likely to be able to spawn successfully.

Clown Killifish *(Pseudoepiplatys annulatus)*

This West African species is also known as the rocket panchax, because of the shape of its body. Its appearance is quite distinctive compared with many killifish since there are four prominent chocolate-brown bands encircling its body, separated by pale yellowish-white areas. Sexing is straightforward, as the male has a brilliant red and blue caudal fin and a yellow area at the front of the dorsal fin. Males are also decidedly larger in size, and have blue eyes.

Livefood must feature prominently in their diet and their aquarium should contain a peat substrate and floating plants.

These killifish show to good effect in a group in a tank on their own; they should not be mixed with aggressive species.

Plants for spawning purposes need to be of the fine-leaved variety. Breeding can present problems however, since the spawn will need to be removed soon after being laid. If the young killifish hatch in the aquarium, they are likely to be eaten by the adults.

Rearing can be difficult, because the fry will not actively hunt for food. Like their parents, they wait for invertebrates to come within reach and then strike out. Gentle circulation of the water is therefore recommended. Avoid adding eggs to an established tank of fry, because when they hatch the young fry are likely to fall victim to their older siblings. Infusoria or a commercial substitute should be used as a first food.

Guenther's Nothobranch *(Nothobranchius guentheri)*

The *Nothobranchius* killifish originate from tropical parts of East Africa, where they often have a very brief seasonal existence. Many of them, such as this species, are highly colourful. In this case, males are larger than females and their coloration is brighter. It is not a good idea to keep males together because they are likely to fight, although this may be avoided in a heavily planted aquarium. The substrate should again consist of peat, where the females will ultimately bury their eggs, and the water level should be relatively low.

Be prepared to carry out partial water changes every 2 weeks or so in order to prevent any significant build-up of nitrogenous waste, as this is likely to be harmful to the fish. Both flake food and assorted livefood will be eaten, with the latter being preferred.

Lowering of the water level in the aquarium promotes spawning activity once these fish are mature. The eggs will be buried in a shallow pit and are then covered over. Remove the adult fish and then allow the remaining water to evaporate. After a period of about 4 months replenish the aquarium using soft water; the fry should then emerge within 4 weeks. Adding a little flake food often helps to trigger the hatching process. Small invertebrates should then be provided for rearing purposes. The killifish grow rapidly and will be mature by 3 months old.

Palmqvist's Nothobranch *(Nothobranchius palmqvisti)*

Originating from the coastal areas of southern Kenya and Tanzania, these killifish can be distinguished by the red patterning on their bodies which, in the case of males, resembles a net. Females lack this patterning, being greyish and also smaller in size. Palmqvist's nothobranch should be kept in a species tank containing plenty of cover, to decrease the risk of aggressive encounters between males. The addition of a little sea salt to their aquarium water can be beneficial. These fish can be at risk from piscine tuberculosis and the parasite known as *Oodinium*.

The spawning tank should be tall and only filled to a depth of a few inches. It is best to use a pad heater and to leave the tank uncovered–the aim being to allow the water to evaporate, with the falling water level triggering spawning activity. The adult fish can then be removed and are likely to die soon afterwards.

The eggs should be treated as recommended for Guenther's nothobranch, and the fry can be reared in a similar fashion. Do not be too hasty to give up if the eggs do not hatch within a few weeks of being returned to the water. It may take 6 months for this process to occur in some cases.

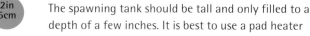
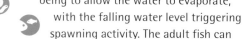
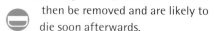

2in
5cm

American Flagfish *(Jordanella floridae)*

The distribution of this fish extends from Florida down to the Mexican province of Yucatan. It occurs in slow moving stretches of water where there is plenty of aquatic vegetation. The black blotch located beneath the dorsal fin is more prominent in female American flagfish. Males are more colourful, with red spots on the body and also on the dorsal fin.

Fine gravel should be used as a substrate in an aquarium for these killifish. Thick areas of fine-leaved plants can be included, along with rocks which may be colonized by algae. This and other greenstuff forms a significant part of the diet of American flagfish, although they will also eat livefood and flake.

Males become especially territorial as the time for spawning approaches and drive the females quite fiercely, so adequate cover is essential to provide retreats at this stage. The eggs, numbering perhaps 70 in total, are finally laid, sometimes over the course of several days, in a hollow in the substrate.

The male will remain with them, fanning them with his fins, but the female should be removed after spawning because she may eat the spawn. Hatching typically occurs after about a week. Fry can be fed on infusoria at first and then moved to a tank where there is plenty of algae when they are about a fortnight old.

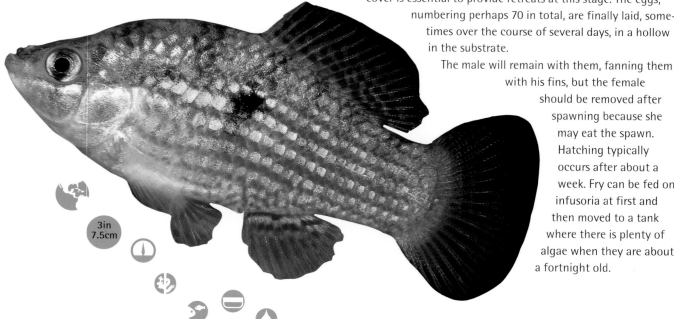

3in
7.5cm

Green Rivulus *(Rivulus urophthalmus)*

Rather confusingly, this species is also known as the golden rivulus on occasions as there are effectively two different colour varieties. The male green rivulus itself is brownish-green, with red dots on the flanks, while females are duller and browner. Females display the characteristic rivulus spot, located on the back of the base of the caudal fin; it is dark in colour with a lighter, narrow band surrounding it. This spot is actually absent in the golden variety, which is of a yellower shade as its name suggests. Females can be easily identified in this case how-ever, since they, unlike males, have no red markings on their fins.

A relatively shallow, well-planted aquarium, preferably with a dark substrate, is ideal for these fish. It is vital that their aquarium is covered however, because rivulus will leap on to floating plants and then slide back into the water later. Regular partial water changes will need to be carried out. A wide variety of foodstuff will be eaten, but livefood tends to be preferred.

As a prelude to successful breeding, the sexes should be separated. These killifish spawn among suitable plants such as *Myriophyllum* and a male can be accommodated with two or three females for this purpose. Spawning is often a protracted process, with the relatively large eggs being laid over the course of a week or more. These should be transferred to a separate tank for hatching, which occurs within 14 days. Fry should be reared with infusoria at first and then brine shrimp *nauplii* can be offered, with the young fish growing rapidly under favourable conditions.

Longfin Killifish *(Pterolebias longipennis)*

The caudal fin of these killifish is well developed, resem-bling a fan in shape, although the dorsal fin is actually much smaller than in many related genera. The fins of the female are also smaller in terms of their overall size. The dominant colour in both sexes is shades of brown, with an iridescence which is marked in the case of the male. Longfin killifish originate from parts of Brazil and neighbouring countries such as Argentina, where they occur in temporary pools of water and so display an annual life-cycle.

These fish have large appetites, particularly for live-food, although they will also eat flake food. Spawning occurs in the substrate and, as with the *Cynolebias* species (see page 90), the eggs must be allowed to dry out for 4 months or so. The peat can be stored in a plastic box out of direct sunlight during this period. There is no need to punch ventilation holes in the lid–this is likely to cause the peat to dry out completely, which is not desirable–just lift the lid briefly every week or so.

Adding rain water to the peat when it is placed back in an aquarium is a good way to encourage some of the fry to emerge. Drying the substrate and repeating the process in due course is recommended however, because not all the fry will hatch on the first occasion. Rotifers can be used as an initial food. The young killifish will grow rapidly and may themselves be mature when only 6 weeks old.

LIVEBEARERS

This popular group of fish offers a great deal of potential, both for the newcomer to tropical fish-keeping and also for the more experienced enthusiast. These fish are also known as livebearing toothcarps. Some, such as the guppy and swordtail, are very well known to aquarists, whereas others are rarely encountered, with stock only generally being available from specialist breeders. The more unusual forms tend to be much duller in coloration compared with the bright, brash appearance of the many strains of domesticated livebearers, such as guppies, that now exist.

Breeding these fish is generally easier than with most egg layers, although the adult fish may again show an unfortunate tendency to eat their fry. Separate tanks are therefore generally recommended, although in a well-planted aquarium at least some fry are likely to escape the jaws of their capricious elders, provided the adult fish are kept well fed.

Guppy *(Poecilia reticulata)*

Today's guppies are far removed in appearance from their wild ancestor, which is believed to have been discovered in about 1865 by the Revd. John Guppy on the Caribbean island of Trinidad. They are generally more colourful and a wide range of fin embellishments, such as sword and delta tail varieties, are now being bred. Patterned forms, such as the king cobra with snake-like markings, are also popular.

Not all the strains which have been developed in the past are widely kept today however, because fashions change and the fertility of highly inbred strains can be low. In many countries, the different varieties of guppy are entered at fish shows where they are judged on their individual characteristics.

Sexing guppies is easy, with females being significantly larger than males and duller in coloration. If possible, choose the biggest females on offer, because they will produce the most offspring. Unfortunately however, having mated once, early in life, the female guppy will be capable of producing several broods in succession. It is therefore vital that young females are kept apart from males until breeding is required or you will be uncertain of the parentage of the offspring.

In the case of mature breeding stock purchased from pet or aquatic shops, the females will already be fertilized. They increase in size and develop a dark patch before giving birth.

Transferring the pregnant female to a separate tank equipped with a breeding trap should ensure that the young guppies survive. If the young are to be reared successfully in a community aquarium, it must be heavily planted or the majority are likely to be eaten soon after birth. A mature female guppy may produce over 100 fry.

1in
2.5cm

Swordtail *(Xiphophorus helleri)*

The name of these popular livebearers stems from the sword-like appearance of the male's caudal fin. However, their appearance has been altered significantly as a result of domestication, both in terms of their coloration and the appearance of their fins. There is, for example, a double sword variant, where both top and bottom parts of the tail fin are elongated. There is also a well-established hi-fin form, recognizable by its greatly enlarged dorsal fin.

The red variety of the swordtail is very striking, in noticeable contrast to the wild fish which is predominantly greenish in colour. Many of the colour variants were developed in Germany and are named after the towns concerned, such as Berlin or Hamburg. A number of these originated from crosses involving the platy (*X. maculatus*)–although swordtails with black speckling characteristic of this strain have subsequently been discovered in the wild, where the species occurs from Mexico south to Guatemala. There are now more than 30 different varieties of the swordtail in existence.

Swordtails are ideal for a community aquarium and will eat a wide variety of foods, including flake, as well as browsing on any algae. Avoid keeping more than one male in the company of females however, because they are often aggressive towards each other and the weaker individuals will be mercilessly bullied. A group of males may actually be more amenable together. It is not a good idea to house swordtails with species known to nip the fins of their companions, such as various barbs, because this could create problems. Their breeding requirements are identical to those of the platy.

Platy *(Xiphophorus maculatus)*

Even in the wild state, the platy shows considerable variation in its coloration through its range, which extends from southern Mexico to Guatemala and Honduras. Males can be distinguished by their smaller size and by the presence of a gonopodium, which is a modification to the anal fin. The resulting tube-like structure enables sperm to be passed from male to female during mating and is characteristically seen in this group of fish because the eggs of livebearers have to be fertilized internally.

Some wild platies show reddish markings, although their natural coloration tends to be olive-brown. Domestication has again resulted in the development of a number of highly colourful varieties, with red often predominating. The addition of a colour food to the diet of these fish, as with other species, can help to emphasize their appeal.

More than 30 different varieties now exist, some of which have black markings on their bodies. The tuxedo platy, for example, has much of the lower part of its body black, with contrasting coloured areas elsewhere. Wagtail platies have black fins and a dark mouth, with their bodies usually being reddish. Changes in fin shape and size have also occurred.

Platies are adaptable fish and they will thrive as part of a community aquarium. They feed on a variety of food, including flake, and are not quarrelsome, even among themselves.

Breeding can be accomplished without difficulty, although for the best results gravid females must be transferred to a separate tank and kept in a breeding trap until the young are born. The female can then be removed and the fry reared on powdered flake food and a suitable commercial food for livebearer fry.

There is another species of platy, called the variegated platy (*X. variatus*), which originates from southern Mexico. It is slightly larger than the platy itself and has a more elongated body. Crossbreeding between these forms has occurred repeatedly and their requirements are identical.

Sailfin Molly *(Poecilia latipinna)*

Although wild mollies are silvery-green, the best known
domesticated strains are black. While their coloration
may not be instantly appealing, these black mollies
can appear stunning when kept under suitable lighting
alongside reddish-orange fish such as platies. There are
now many other colour varieties of molly, ranging
from the silvery coloured platinum through to shades
of yellow and marbled chocolate types. Lyre-tailed
individuals are also quite common today.

   Mollies normally live in brackish water and can
benefit from the addition of a small amount of
aquarium salt to their tank. They may otherwise be
more susceptible to fungal infections, although they
are generally robust fish. Active fish by nature, it is not
unknown for them to leap out of an uncovered
aquarium, usually with catastrophic consequences.

   Male sailfin mollies swim with their dorsal fin held
erect while their anal fin is modified into a rod,
called the gonopodium, which conveys
sperm during mating. Females may produce
over 80 offspring at a time. The young mollies
must be given adequate space as they develop or
they will not grow as large as might be hoped,
although in other respects they will remain healthy.

   The upturned mouth of the fish indicates that they prefer to

4in
10cm

feed at the water's surface, rather
than in the lower reaches of the
tank, but they will browse happily on most algae, as well as
eating formulated foods.

Black Molly *(Poecilia sphenops)*

The wild form of this fish is very different in appearance to its
domesticated relative, being an attractive shade of bluish-
green with yellow dots on its flanks. Females are again larger in
size and lack the gonopodium of the male. It is widely
distributed, from Texas southwards through Central America
to Colombia. These mollies occur in a range of habitats, including brackish water, and the addition of marine salt to their
aquarium is recommended; the amount of salt added will
depend on the water in which they were previously kept,
but it should result in a 5–7% solution.

4in
10cm

   The pointed-mouth molly was first kept in Germany
back in 1899, at a very early stage in the history of the
tropical aquarium hobby. Hybridization with related
species such as *P. velifera* then led to the appearance of
the black form now known as the black molly in 1909.
Some display an orange band on the edge of the
caudal fin.

   Care needs to be taken when purchasing mollies,
because they are very susceptible to the
parasitic ailment known as
white spot (see page 21). If
one individual in a tank is
infected, the likelihood
is that the others
there will be
equally at risk.
Mollies are useful
for controlling algae in the
aquarium. They will feed mainly
on plant matter, so vegetation
should be relatively hardy. Greenstuff can
feature in their diet along with other foods such as
flake. Breeding follows the pattern of that of the sailfin molly
and mature females produce broods quite regularly, often
every six weeks or so.

Hump-backed Limia *(Limia nigrofasciata)*

The distinctive hump of these fish is only evident in mature males. They are also sometimes described as black-barred limias, as a series of dark vertical bands transverse their flanks. These markings are broader and less numerous in females.

The hump-backed limia occurs on the Caribbean island of Hispaniola. In aquarium surroundings, these fish feed on a variety of livefood, tablets and flake. They can be kept in brackish water and suitable plants should be included to give a fairly dense covering of vegetation, especially at the sides and back of the tank.

These livebearers breed quite readily, but it is important to keep the female separate from her brood because she is likely to eat them. Separation can be achieved by means of a breeding trap. The hump-backed limia generally produces relatively large broods, often comprising 50 fry, compared with other *Limia* species. The young will feed readily on brine shrimp *nauplii*.

If the female is herself well fed, broods can be anticipated every month or so. Interestingly, it appears that the percentage of male fry increases as the water temperature rises. As the males then approach maturity, their dorsal fin undergoes a dramatic increase in size, and the characteristic hump soon develops.

Mosquito Fish *(Heterandria formosa)*

This tiny fish is one of the smallest species in the world. It originates from south-eastern areas of the USA and is the most northerly representative of its genus. Males are notably smaller than females and show the typical modification of the anal fin into a gonopodium. As their name suggests, mosquito fish benefit from a diet comprising small livefood, including mosquito larvae, although they also eat various dry foods.

The water temperature in their aquarium should be reasonably low, ranging from as low as 61°F (16°C) up to a maximum of 77°F (25°C). Dense vegetation, including floating plants, is recommended.

The breeding behaviour of this species is unique, since the young are born over the course of 2 weeks or so rather than in a short space of time as with other livebearers. In some cases, this period can be significantly protracted, lasting for over 2 months.

     Mosquito fish are not especially prolific, producing a maximum of about 50 offspring in a brood. The young fish grow rapidly and are unlikely to be molested by the female, especially if there is sufficient cover in the aquarium where they can hide from any danger. In view of their size, mosquito fish are best housed in a species tank, rather than as part of a community aquarium.

Two-spot Livebearer *(Heterandria bimaculata)*

There is a distinct difference in appearance between the fish of this species found in mountainous areas and those which occur in waters at lower altitude. The upland forms are an iridescent greenish-brown and are quite stout, whereas others from lowland areas carry much greater speckling on their bodies, with dark edges to the individual scales, and have a more streamlined shape. In both cases there is a prominent black spot on each side of the body at the base of the caudal fin.

The two-spot livebearer ranges from Mexico southwards into parts of Guatemala, Honduras and Belize. Females can be easily distinguished because they are nearly twice as large as males of this species and lack the red edge present on their caudal fin.

The two-spot livebearer is an aggressive species which needs to be fed on livefood, although other items such as flake food may be eaten. A well-planted aquarium, with clean, oxygenated water is essential. Breeding is frequently achieved successfully in such surroundings, provided that the fry can be protected from their rapacious parents. Over 100 may be produced at a single spawning, with the young being produced between a month and 6 weeks following mating.

Halfbeak *(Dermogenys pusillus)*

The majority of halfbeaks are marine fish. This particular species inhabits both fresh and brackish areas of water however, being widely distributed from south-east Asia to the Great Sunda Islands. A number of subspecies have been identified through its range and there can be some variation in appearance between individuals as a result.

Males can be identified in all cases by their smaller size however, and a distinctive red area on the dorsal fin. The alternative name of wrestling halfbeak comes from their habit of locking jaws and trying to overpower their opponent. Such combat can last for perhaps 30 minutes and the combatants may be injured. If their rather delicate long lower jaws are damaged, these fish may no longer be able to eat. It is therefore recommended that males are kept on their own, in the company of several females.

An aquarium for halfbeaks should be relatively shallow, as they will spend most of their time near the surface, with some floating plants but also areas of clear water where they can swim. The addition of some marine salt to the tank may be beneficial for these fish.

Livefood such as wingless fruit flies and hatchling crickets should feature prominently in their diet, and the latter can be treated with a special balancer to make up for any vitamin and mineral deficiencies. The benefits of this are likely to become apparent in the breeding period. Females often produce a high percentage of stillborn young, but this situation is improved when a more balanced diet is provided. Up to 40 fry are likely, with mature females breeding every month or two.

Young halfbeaks, measuring about 0.4in (1cm) long, must be reared on small livefood. When transferred to new surroundings these fish are often nervous and may hurt themselves by swimming at the glass of the aquarium. Sticking strips of paper on the outside will indicate the presence of a barrier; heavy planting around the sides should also help to prevent injuries.

Butterfly Goodeid *(Ameca splendens)*

This relatively stocky species originates from waters in the upland areas of central Mexico. As with most other live-bearers, females are decidedly larger than males, being about 1in (2.5cm) longer on average. Pairs can also be recognized by their coloration; males are more colourful and show greater iridescence than females. In addition, the male has a more rounded dorsal fin than the female and he has a distinctive notch in his anal fin.

Butterfly goodeids are mainly vegetarian in their feeding habits, although it may be possible to persuade them to take livefood as well on occasions-mosquito larvae are usually the most acceptable form.

In contrast to most other livebearers, female butterfly good-eids are unable to store sperm. This means that they must mate on each occasion prior to the birth of fry; their eggs are otherwise shed, unfertilized, from their bodies. It is quite normal for females to swell up and appear rather distorted when carrying young; this is not a sign of dropsy or another ailment.

The gestation period in these fish is relatively long and can last for up to 2 months. As many as 50 fry may be produced, each measuring up to 0.5in (1.25cm) long. They can be reared on a commercial livefood diet and are not normally at risk of being eaten by their parents.

When the fry are born, they do not have a protective egg case around them which splits at birth. They are nourished internally in their mother's body, confirming that these fish are truly viviparous, rather than oviparous, like most livebearers. Unfortunately, in spite of their interesting habits, they are not commonly available.

Knife Livebearer *(Alfaro cultratus)*

The knife-like serrations present on the underside of the body of these fish, extending forward from the base of the tail, are responsible for their common name. Knife livebearers originate from Costa Rica, Guatemala, Nicaragua and Panama, where they inhabit fast flowing streams. They therefore require well-aerated, clean water in aquarium surroundings. The addition of a small amount of sea salt may be beneficial.

The rod-like structure of the male's gonopodium provides an easy way to distinguish the sexes; the anal fins of the slightly larger female are shaped rather like a fan. Their bodies are semi-transparent, with yellow markings apparent on the fins, and the edges are bluish.

Knife livebearers prefer to feed on small livefood such as mosquito larvae, although they can be persuaded to eat flake as well. Shy by nature, these fish should be housed in a densely planted aquarium. Raising the water temperature to about 82°F (28°C) once the fish are well established is likely to trigger breeding activity.

The young, numbering up to 100, are born about 2 months after mating, and care needs to be taken that they are not immediately consumed by their parents. Repeated breedings every 5 weeks or so may be expected, with the young knife livebearers being mature themselves at a year old.

CATFISH

There are more than 2000 different types of catfish, divided into 20 families. They have an extensive worldwide distribution and show tremendous diversity in both size and shape. Members of this group of fish are rarely colourful, but they frequently arouse comment because of their bizarre appearance. They have sensory barbels around the mouth which may be several inches long in some cases, and which help them to find their food. Those with the longest barbels are usually predatory by nature.

Catfish lack the typical scales seen in other fish. Instead, they have an armoured body covering consisting of bony plates or, alternatively, thick skin protected by a coating of mucus. A number of species also have protective spines on exposed parts of their bodies. As many catfish are slow swimmers, they rely on camouflage to escape detection during the daytime and then become more active at dusk. They often occupy the lower part of the aquarium and have a reputation for being valuable scavengers, but catfish should not be expected to survive solely on algae or the leftover food of other fish.

Bronze Corydoras *(Corydoras aeneus)*

These small catfish are very easy to cater for in an aquarium. They are also quite likely to breed, provided that their eggs are not eaten by the other tank occupants. The natural form of this fish has a reddish-brown hue, resembling bronze. Other varieties, including an albino form with a pure white body and red eyes, have been developed by fishkeepers.

In the wild, bronze corydoras are widely distributed in northern South America, from the Caribbean island of Trinidad southwards to Brazil. There is some variation in their appearance through their huge range. There is one type which has gold streaks on its head and although this variety has been bred by aquarists, it is not as readily available as the more common form.

3in
7.5cm

These catfish will rest on any wood decorating the bottom of the aquarium or on the gravel. They require a diet based on animal foods, often relishing some of the frozen items now available, such as bloodworm, that must be thawed before use. Small pieces of prawn are also a favoured item in their diet.

For breeding purposes, it is best to keep bronze corydoras in trios comprising one male and two females. Females tend to be larger than males, but it is not a good idea to rely entirely on this distinction when purchasing fish as their size can be influenced by other factors such as age. Males may sometimes have more pointed pelvic fins.

Elegant Corydoras *(Corydoras elegans)*

Corydoras catfish are widely distributed in South America, from Trinidad and Venezuela southwards to Argentina. This particular species inhabits the region of central Amazonia. With in excess of 100 different corydoras already known to science, and new species still being discovered, it is unfortunately not always easy to distinguish between the different forms.

The upper part of the body of the elegant corydoras is dark, especially on the head, while the underparts have a greyish-pink tone. Blackish speckling is often apparent on the fins, with similar markings being present on the body. Sexing is quite difficult, although males tend to display brighter colouring than females.

This corydoras catfish will spend most of its time on the floor of the aquarium and the gravel here must be clean to prevent any infection of the barbels. Males may also prove to be territorial, adopting retreats such as sunken flowerpots, and can become aggressive when a female is ready to spawn.

Their eggs are often attached to the underside of leaves of aquatic plants such as cryptocorynes, and up to 350 may be laid in batches of up to 25 eggs. Hatching is likely to take about 3 days and the young can be reared on rotifers and brine shrimp *nauplii*. They themselves will be able to breed at the age of 10 months.

Peppered Corydoras *(Corydoras paleatus)*

This catfish originates from slow flowing stretches of water in parts of southern Brazil and northern Argentina. As a result, it could benefit from being kept at a slightly cooler temperature than those originating close to the equator, around 64–68°F (18–20°C).

Dark brownish markings set against a paler yellowish background and bluish-green iridescence around the head help to distinguish this species. There is a relatively rare 'albino' form which retains these darker areas, helping to distinguish it from the similar form of the bronze corydoras. A dark patch at the front of the dorsal fin is a consistent feature.

Discovered by the famous zoologist Charles Darwin, the peppered corydoras can be sexed when mature with females being larger than males and having shorter, less pointed dorsal fins. The colour of the female underparts assumes a pinkish hue as the time for spawning approaches and it is often recommended that two males are included with a female to give the maximum likelihood of achieving breeding success. Feeding a high-protein diet for a fortnight beforehand and

lowering the temperature of the water by about 10°F (5°C) can serve to encourage spawning.

Eggs are released in the upper part of the tank in batches, or may be deposited on the leaves of plants. Around 300 in total comprise a typical spawning. Hatching is then likely to occur within a week, although this period may be prolonged occasionally.

Bearded Corydoras *(Corydoras barbatus)*

This corydoras is one of the larger members of the group. It originates from Brazil where it occurs in relatively cold water, around 68°F (20°C), living on the base of streams and rivers, scurrying under plants if danger threatens. The markings of these corydoras are especially striking and may vary somewhat between individuals. Males are more colourful and have bristles around their mouth, which is why this species is known as the bearded corydoras.

An aquarium for these catfish should have a layer of sand on its base so they can burrow, along with other retreats such as flowerpots and rocky areas. Livefood and the addition of peat to the filter should help to encourage spawning activity. The pair will adopt the typical T-shaped position associated with these catfish when mating, with the female often appearing to be aggressive at first.

Spawning may take an hour, during which time the female may produce nearly 150 eggs. Hatching typically takes about 4 days, with the young catfish starting to seek food for the first time when they are almost a week old. Brine shrimp *nauplii* can be offered at this stage and should help to ensure a rapid rate of growth. Repeated spawnings, every month or so, can be anticipated once females start to lay.

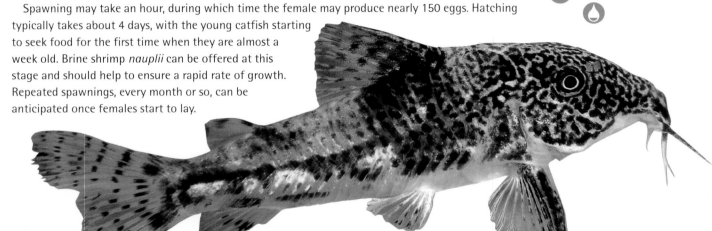

Harald Shultz's Corydoras *(Corydoras haraldshultzi)*

Described for the first time in 1962, Harald Shultz's corydoras is a Brazilian species. It is similar in appearance to another species from this area, known as *C. sterbai*. A series of black dots and small stripes run in lines down the sides of its body and extend across the fins. Those on the caudal fin tend to be closer together and can give the impression of vertical stripes. The underparts are pinkish, with females becoming more swollen in appearance as the time for spawning approaches.

This corydoras is named after the famous late Brazilian fish exporter, Harald Shultz, whose enthusiasm led to a number of today's popular species, including the discus, becoming well known around the world. His family is still involved in the business today and their name is commemorated in other species, including *Corydoras schwartzi* discovered at the mouth of the Rio Purus in the Amazonas region of Brazil.

The care of the Harald Shultz corydoras is similar to that of related *Corydoras* species, with an assortment of livefood forming the preferred basis of their diet. Corydoras feed essentially on the floor of the aquarium and are often valued as scavengers, but they will benefit from being provided with their own specific foods.

Blue Corydoras *(Corydoras natterei)*

Originating from rivers around the Brazilian city of Rio de Janeiro, in the south of the country, this species is also sometimes described as Natterer's corydoras. It has a distinctive bluish-green iridescence along the sides of its body, which is responsible for its more usual common name.

The blue corydoras has proved to be an easy species to maintain and spawn, although it prefers relatively low temperatures between 68°F and 75°F (20–24°C). In common with other members of this genus, the armour-like pattern of scales is clearly apparent on the sides of the body. The more rounded shape of females, especially prior to spawning, provides an easy means of distinguishing the sexes, although this is not critical in any event since these are quite social fish and can be kept in small groups.

A spawning tank is advisable however, because these catfish will consume their eggs if left with them. Spawning may occur over several days, and keeping the adult fish well fed through this period should help to ensure that the majority of the eggs are left unmolested.

When mating the male holds the female briefly by the barbels, grasping her with his pectoral fin. She lays a group of eggs that are cupped together and which pass into her ventral fins. Fertilization is effected when she carries the eggs through the male's output of sperm. The fry of the blue corydoras are relatively easy to rear on an initial diet of brine shrimp *nauplii* once they are free-swimming.

Pygmy Catfish *(Corydoras pygmaeus)*

One of the smaller members of the *Corydoras* group, this catfish tends to spend less time at the bottom of the tank than many related species and is a more active swimmer. It originates from waterways in Brazil and Peru. Pygmy catfish occur in shoals comprising thousands of fish in the wild and must be kept together in groups in aquarium surroundings. They can be housed in the company of other small, non-aggressive fish such as neon tetras (see page 43).

These catfish eat a wide variety of foods, often searching for food on the leaves of plants growing in their aquarium. Livefood such as mosquito larvae will be consumed readily, along with regular catfish food.

Spawning is most likely to be successful in the winter period, at least in the northern hemisphere, with the water temperature being lowered to about 72°F (22°C) at this stage. Males can again be recognized by their slimmer profiles, and two males should be housed with a single female.

Eggs are laid on plants in the spawning tank, with *Hygrophila polysperma* being favoured.

Hatching takes about 3 days, with the eggs darkening in colour through this period. The young will start feeding after a similar interval.

Keep the water level in the rearing quarters relatively low so they will be able to find their food, such as brine shrimp *nauplii*, without difficulty.

Regular weekly water changes will be essential as the young catfish grow.

Leopard Corydoras *(Corydoras julii)*

Found in the tributaries of the lower Amazon in Brazil, these attractively patterned catfish have silvery bodies and small black dots which may coalesce into lines, notably in the vicinity of the head. There is a more definite black stripe running down the centre of the body to the base of the caudal fin. The leopard corydoras is often confused with the Peruvian species known as *C. trilineatus*. Both these fish have a striped appearance, but the spotting on the leopard corydoras is finer and more delicate.

Like other *Corydoras* species, these make lively occupants within a community aquarium and they are also active during the day. Members of this genus are able to breathe atmospheric air directly and the fact that they may be seen swallowing air at the water's surface is not a cause for concern. Corydoras can absorb oxygen from the rear part of their gut, which helps them to survive either in very shallow stretches of water or where the oxygen content is low. It is important to ensure that the substrate in the aquarium does not become stale however, because this can trigger skin infections.

Green Catfish *(Brochis spendens)*

The appearance of the *Brochis* catfish is very similar to that of Corydoras, although its dorsal fin consists of more rays and it has a relatively flattened body shape. This particular species is also sometimes described as the emerald catfish, because of the iridescent green coloration on its flanks, and used to be known under the scientific name of *B. coeruleus*. It originates from the upper part of the Amazon, in parts of Peru, Ecuador and Brazil.

Sand should be used to form at least part of the substrate, and the aquarium should include bogwood as well as being well planted so that the fish have a range of retreats. Regular water changes and a clean substrate are vital for the health of these catfish. They can be fed on a standard catfish food, augmented with fresh items such as small pieces of prawn.

These catfish will not be destructive towards plants.

Female green catfish are slightly larger in size, with more pinkish underparts than the male. Livefood is very important for conditioning purposes, while the spawning tank itself should be bare apart from a covering of floating plants, such as *Ricca fluitans*, at the surface.

A group of three males and two females is often recommended to achieve successful spawning. Each female is likely to produce up to 300 eggs, many of which will be sprinkled in the floating plants. Those which fall to the bottom are unlikely to be eaten.

Dwarf Sucking Catfish *(Otocinclus affinis)*

These small catfish live well in a mixed aquarium, but they do appear to require plants if they are to thrive in these surroundings. This species originates from the south-east of Brazil, occurring in the vicinity of Rio de Janeiro. They can be distinguished by their golden flanks and long brownish-black stripes extending down the sides of the body.

Members of this genus are highly valued for keeping algal growth under control in the aquarium; the potential drawback is that these catfish may also decide to eat some other plant matter. Green food and other sources of algae, such as spirulina, can be included in their diet, along with some livefood and regular catfish food.

Males may be distinguished by their slender shape. For most of the time these catfish are relatively inactive, hanging on to plants or the glass of the aquarium using their sucker mouths. At the start of the spawning period however, they will swim very rapidly, darting on to broad leaves where ultimately the eggs are deposited.

The breeding habits of this particular species are similar to those of *Corydoras* species, with the female catching her eggs in her ventral fins, whereas some other *Otocinclus* lay directly

on to the plant leaves. Up to 100 eggs may be produced in batches in this fashion, with the fry hatching about 3 days later. They anchor themselves with their sucker mouths, and will remain relatively inert for a further 3 days until the yolk sac is absorbed. Rotifers and egg yolk have been used successfully as rearing foods at this stage. The water must be well aerated and partial changes carried out weekly as the young catfish grow.

Glass Catfish *(Kryptopterus bicirrhis)*

Most of the skeletal structure of this catfish is visible through its transparent body, although its body organs are contained within a silvery reflective sac behind the head. These fish are highly social and should only be kept in groups. They are active by nature and must have adequate space for swimming in their aquarium, which should not be brightly lit. Plants are best confined to the sides and back of the tank.

The water temperature should be maintained at around 77°F (25°C), especially in the case of newly purchased fish of

this species, or they are likely to succumb to white spot (see page 21). It is probably better to keep glass catfish on their own, but they can be mixed successfully with non-aggressive companions which will not disturb them. These fish prefer to feed on livefood such as mosquito larvae and will not scavenge on the floor of their aquarium, unlike many catfish. They can usually be persuaded to accept dry food when necessary.

Unfortunately, it is impossible to sex glass catfish visually, although males may be smaller. The shimmering colours that can sometimes be detected on the sides of their bodies are dependent on the aquarium lighting, rather than being an indication of their gender. Breeding in these surroundings has yet to be accomplished in any event.

African Glass Catfish *(Eutropiellus debauwi)*

This species can be easily distinguished by the three dark stripes running down the sides of its body, which become more prominent in older fish. These markings are paler in the case of females. The central stripe extends down into the caudal fin.

Like their Asian counterparts, these glass catfish are active fish which need to be kept in groups. They can be mixed with other, non-aggressive species. Livefoods are favoured, but they will also eat dry food. African glass catfish originate from the Congo basin and will benefit from having some movement of water in their aquarium. They are unlikely to damage any plants and must be given adequate space for swimming. The lighting should be relatively subdued, with floating plants helping to provide areas of shade.

Very little is known about the breeding habits of these catfish. Females may be easier to identify as the time for spawning approaches, since they swell in size. Their eggs are laid individually on plants. If spawning does occur in aquarium surroundings, it is advisable to move the eggs to a separate tank for hatching, because the female catfish shows no interest in them after laying. Once the fry are free-swimming, typical rearing foods such as brine shrimp *nauplii* should be offered to them.

Two-spot Catfish *(Mystus micracanthus)*

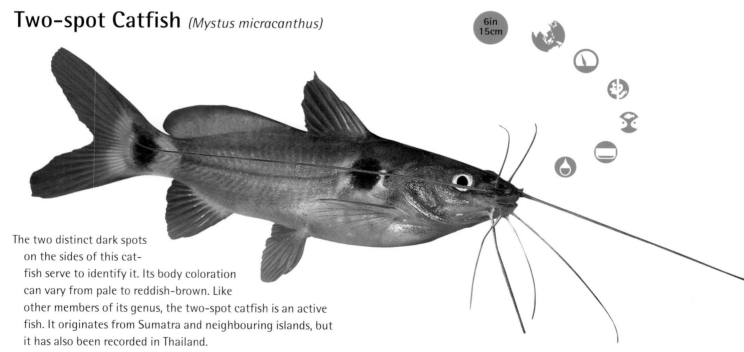

The two distinct dark spots on the sides of this catfish serve to identify it. Its body coloration can vary from pale to reddish-brown. Like other members of its genus, the two-spot catfish is an active fish. It originates from Sumatra and neighbouring islands, but it has also been recorded in Thailand.

These catfish are predatory by nature and will consume not just invertebrates but also smaller fish on occasions. Nevertheless, if accommodated with other fish of similar size, they will not molest them. Gouramis are often recommended as suitable companions. Two-spot catfish have long barbels and use these after dark to seek out food, usually close to the floor of the aquarium. Worms of various types are a favoured food, although they will also take pieces of shrimp quite readily. They should be housed in a relatively spacious aquarium which provides them with plenty of space for swimming purposes.

It does not appear possible to sex these catfish easily, and spawning is far from commonplace in aquarium surroundings. Placing a group of females with a male, which has a more slender appearance, in an aquarium where the water temperature is lowered to 68°F (20°C) may be successful. Their relatively large eggs may be scattered around the tank soon afterwards in the morning, with the resulting fry being reared on small livefoods.

Banded Siamese Catfish *(Leiocassis siamensis)*

These hardy, interesting catfish first became known in the
aquarium hobby during the 1950s. They originate from
Thailand, where they are widely distributed, even sometimes
being found in brackish waters. Their underparts are yellow,
while most of the body is blackish or dark brown with several
irregular bands running down the sides. These markings help to
conceal the presence of these catfish when they are resting
during the day.

   Small specimens of banded Siamese catfish may be housed in
a mixed collection of fish. However, larger individuals must not
be mixed, as smaller companions are likely to be seized and
eaten whole and bigger fish may suffer fin damage if attacked.
Shrimp and bloodworm should form part of their regular diet,
and they may also be persuaded to eat pellets.

   A well-planted aquarium is ideal for these catfish. When resting, they may
choose to lie on their backs; this is not a sign of illness, but normal behaviour
in this species. They can also make a repeated croaking sound. Males are often larger and
although banded Siamese catfish are reluctant to spawn in an aquarium this has been achieved on occasions.

6in
15cm

   The eggs are likely to be laid close to the substrate, in among aquatic plants there. Hatching is likely to take
3 days, during which time the spawn is guarded by the male. The fry will be free-swimming after a similar
interval and should then be reared on their own.

Upside-down Catfish *(Synodontis contractus)*

Although not especially attractive in terms of its coloration,
being mainly brownish with dark blotches, the upside-down
catfish is an unusual aquarium occupant. It is adept at swimming on its back, as its name suggests, and the usual colour
pattern of lighter underparts is then reversed. Upside-down
catfish feed readily in this position, seizing floating food from
the surface or grasping algae. Any aquarium snails will not be
safe in the company of these fish.

   Upside-down catfish originate from Zaire, occurring in large
shoals in weedy stretches of water. They should be kept in
groups in an aquarium. The lighting should be very subdued as
these fish dislike bright light; the appearance of three vertical
bands down the sides of their bodies is indicative of stress,
often for this reason. These catfish are primarily nocturnal and
will need hiding places where they can retreat during the day.

   Spawning has proved to be difficult to achieve in aquarium
surroundings. Females can be distinguished at this stage by
their more rotund appearance however, and the eggs are likely
to be concealed in a dark locality
in the aquarium. Hatching will
take about a week and the fry
will be swimming in a normal
fashion in a further 3 days,
eating brine shrimp *nauplii*.
Based on observations of
the young of a very similar
species called *S. nigroventris*,
which is also known as the
upside-down catfish, the fry
are only likely to start
swimming on their backs
from the age of 10 weeks
onwards. These two catfish
can be distinguished since
S. nigroventris has a smaller head
and eyes than this species.

3in
7.5cm

Polka-dot Catfish *(Synodontis angelicus)*

The striking white spots set against the black body coloration make an attractive combination in young polka-dot catfish. As these fish grow older however, the contrast fades and their bodies become greyer. Females gain a more rounded profile as they mature.

Polka-dot catfish originate from Zaire and the Cameroons. They will often excavate in the floor covering of their aquarium, so it may be better to set plants here in pots to prevent them from being uprooted. Bogwood should be included, to provide additional cover. These catfish are essentially nocturnal and are relatively inactive during the day. Polka-dot catfish will eat algae in the tank, and other sources such as spirulina can be provided as part of their diet. They will also eat small livefood and, occasionally, catfish pellets.

Regular water changes every fortnight or so will be essential to prevent any accumulation of nitrates in the aquarium, which is likely to be harmful. These catfish are not particularly aggressive and can be housed in the company of other fish of similar size. They are quite social by nature and can be kept in a group as well; this gives the greatest likelihood of spawning success, although little is known about their reproductive behaviour.

Whip-tailed Catfish *(Rineloricaria filamentosa)*

There is a long whip-like filament extending from the top of the caudal fin of these catfish, which is responsible for their common name. Their coloration varies quite widely, being shades of brown, with dark areas on the front rays of the dorsal fin serving to identify this species from related forms. Males have bristles on the sides of their heads, which extend to their pectoral fins.

This species is found in the River Magdalena, with other members of the genus widely distributed in clear, fast flowing waters across northern and central parts of South America. Distinguishing between them can be difficult, but all require similar care.

Well-oxygenated, clean water is essential for whip-tailed catfish, with regular water changes every fortnight or so being necessary. These catfish also require rock-work such as slate, bogwood and plants to provide cover. They are not aggressive, but need a spacious aquarium in view of their large size. Both invertebrates and green food should feature as part of their diet.

A pair will clean their chosen spawning area prior to egg laying and lie in the hollow. As many as 200 eggs may be laid by the female, and subsequently her partner will care for them until they hatch about 9 days later. He uses his fins to circulate water over the eggs and then helps the young fry to emerge by sucking at the egg sacs. The water level should be kept low to ensure the fry have no difficulty in finding their food, which can consist of small invertebrates at this stage. Keeping the water clean is essential for the wellbeing of the young catfish.

Twig Catfish *(Farlowella gracilis)*

These strange, slender catfish really do look like twigs when viewed from above. They are predominantly brown in colour, later becoming much paler on the underparts with a broken dark streak running down the sides of their bodies. This provides them with good camouflage in their native habitat, which is the rivers of northern South America. Their slender body shape and pointed head has also led to them being known as needle fish.

Twig catfish are not aggressive by nature and they can be housed with other peaceful species, but you will need a reasonably large aquarium in order to accommodate them properly. The water in the tank needs to be heated to about 75°F (24°C). The interior of their quarters should be decorated with slate and bogwood, firmly positioned in the tank, to provide some hiding places.

Feeding is reasonably straightforward. Twig catfish will browse on any algae growing in the aquarium as they are vegetarian by nature. Feed them on a suitable vegetarian based diet in pelleted form. Pellets will sink readily to the bottom of the aquarium, where these fish will spend most of their time, but take care to avoid overfeeding. If you see the fish poking their noses out above the surface of the water, this is a sign that all is not well in terms of water quality. These catfish normally inhabit fast flowing streams and require well-oxygenated water.

Sexing is reasonably straightforward in mature twig catfish as males develop bristles on their snouts. A pair may breed successfully in aquarium surroundings with the slate in the tank serving as a surface on which the female can lay her eggs.

8in
20cm

Ornate Pimelodus *(Pimelodus ornatus)*

A white band separates the black stripes running down the upper side of the body of this catfish. A third, broad band extends from the front of the dorsal fin down between the pectoral and pelvic fins. When mature, these catfish are relatively large. They are active by nature, and nocturnal. They range from Guyana as far south as Paraguay. Large cichlids and other catfish of similar size make suitable aquarium companions for them.

10in
25cm

The ornate pimelodus needs a shaded aquarium, with suitable daytime hiding places. It will usually remain close to the floor of the tank, but if the oxygen level becomes low it will surface regularly to breathe atmospheric air. Air can be absorbed through the intestinal tract although this should not be encouraged.

Worms of various types, starting with tubifex when young and progressing to earthworms, should feature prominently in their diet. These catfish will also feed on other invertebrates however, taking river shrimp when larger. Nothing is presently known about their breeding habits.

Porthole Catfish *(Dianema longibarbis)*

Whereas many fish have their barbels tucked under their jaws, those of the porthole catfish are prominent, protruding in front of the mouth. This species occurs in the upper reaches of the Amazon from Peru and Brazil. It can be separated from the closely related flag-tail porthole catfish (*D. urostriata*) by its unmarked, transparent caudal fin.

The care of these catfish is quite straightforward, although they are best kept in groups rather than on their own. They are not generally predatory, but they may eat smaller companions on occasions. A well-planted tank will suit them well as, like many catfish, they hide away during the day and become more active after dark. Porthole catfish are able to hold their position in water simply by vibrating their fins without actually swimming forwards.

Their breeding habits are fascinating; they construct a bubble nest for their eggs. Raising the water temperature to about 82°F (28°C) may serve to trigger this behaviour, although successes are rare in aquarium surroundings. Females may be distinguished from males by their more rotund appearance, particularly prior to spawning.

Clown Peckoltia *(Peckoltia vittata)*

These small suckermouth catfish originate from Brazil, and they will make an attractive addition to any community aquarium which contains small fish. The clown peckoltia is invariably attractively marked, although there can be significant differences in appearance between individuals in this respect. Stripes may predominate in some cases, whereas other fish are more spotted.

Bogwood and stones should be included as part of the aquarium decor for these catfish. They will also utilize submerged clay flowerpots as hiding places during the daytime. Clown plecs, as these fish are sometimes known, become active towards dusk and can prove to be rather territorial. Although they feed primarily on algae, they will not harm plants growing in the aquarium. It is perhaps better to wait until an aquarium is reasonably well established, with a good growth of algae, before purchasing these fish. They may sometimes be reluctant to sample substitute foods, although spirulina can be valuable if they can be persuaded to eat it.

Male clown plecs are believed to be brighter in colour and slightly smaller in size than females, although this may be influenced by their area of distribution. Unfortunately, nothing is currently known about their spawning habits.

Blue-eyed Panaque *(Panaque suttoni)*

The unusual blue eyes of this fish are highly distinctive and make a strong contrast with its dark body. It occurs in northern South America, where it is found in Colombia. Check the condition of these fish carefully prior to purchase, as thin individuals may have been deprived of the opportunity to eat algae and will have lost condition as a result. It may be possible to correct this state of affairs by offering foods such as bloodworm and earthworms, which will also be eaten by these fish, although greenstuff must figure prominently in their diet. Spinach, thawed deep frozen or fresh peas, cress and lettuce are all possible options.

Blue-eyed panaques or plecs require a large aquarium, which should incorporate bogwood and suitable retreats. They are territorial and so must not become overcrowded as they grow because this will lead to conflict. These catfish are not aggressive towards other species however and can be kept with other fish which will not molest them.

It is possible to sex blue-eyed panaques without difficulty, once they are mature, as males develop bristles on their pectoral spines. Breeding details for these fish are basically unknown however, with spawning in aquarium surroundings being most unlikely.

12in
30cm

Sucking Catfish *(Hypostomus punctatus)*

Found in southern parts of Brazil, the sucking catfish is another relatively large member of the suckermouth family *Loricariidae*. Its mouth, which is located under its body, contains teeth which are used for scraping algae off a variety of surfaces. The sucker-like action of its lips also enables this fish to anchor itself firmly on to rocks when, for example, it is faced with a strong current.

A unique feature of this group of fish, found in no other vertebrates, is the presence of a lobe in the iris of each eye, which can be moved into the pupil to control the amount of light entering in. Normally, in other cases, the diameter of the pupils is altered to achieve this effect.

The care of this species does not differ significantly from that of the blue-eyed plec, with the description of 'plec' often being used for all suckermouth catfish rather than just those belonging to the genus *Plecostomus*. The addition of a trace of marine salt to the aquarium is often recommended when settling in newly acquired fish. In spite of their feeding habits, these catfish will generally only eat algae and will not harm the plants that are growing in their quarters.

10in
25cm

Banjo Catfish *(Bunocephalus coracoideus)*

These popular catfish have a wide area of distribution, ranging through the Amazon region as far south as Uruguay. They should be kept in an aquarium with a sandy bottom so that they can bury themselves in the substrate. These catfish will actually force water through their gills to assist their movement when swimming. They are so called because of their distinctive body shape, which resembles a banjo, and are largely nocturnal by nature.

Small crustaceans and various worms are popular food items, although these catfish may also eat pellets and may decide to prey on snails in their aquarium. Sexing is difficult, although males may be slimmer than females, particularly as the time for spawning approaches. It has proved possible to breed them in aquaria, with the male excavating a hollow in the substrate to accommodate what can be as many as 5000 eggs. He then guards them until the fry hatch, about 3 days later. Rotifers have been used to rear the young banjo catfish at first, after which they can be introduced to tubifex worms.

5in
12.5cm

Temminck's Bristlenose *(Ancistrus temmincki)*

The bristlenose catfish are generally distinguished by the presence of tentacles on the front of their head, which are often more prominent and branched in the case of males. These have a sensory value for these bottom-dwelling fish. Bristlenose catfish feed primarily on algae and will consume large quantities, with a single individual being capable of eliminating this growth from a 36in (91cm) aquarium with a light above. Greenstuff should feature in their diet as well, along with vegetarian foods.

Temminck's bristlenose is found in clear, turbulent streams and rivers feeding the Amazon in northern South America, and it requires similar well-oxygenated moving water in aquarium surroundings. These fish will anchor on to rocks or other tank decor using their suckermouths.

6in
15cm

Spawning has been possible by providing retreats such as plastic or bamboo tubes weighed down in the tank. Their eggs are an unmistakable orange colour and are looked after by the male. As many as 200 may result from a single spawning. Hatching is likely to take 5 days and for the next week or so the fry anchor themselves within the tube.

Stick to vegetarian foods at this stage; powdered flake food can be used along with a suitable fry food for rearing purposes. Wood should always be available in the aquarium as these catfish seem not to thrive without access to it. They will rasp the surface of the wood and ingest particles; this may be a dietary need, or it could assist them in maintaining their teeth in good condition.

Chocolate Catfish *(Acanthodoras spinosissimus)*

This species is also sometimes known as the talking catfish because of the way in which it croaks when lifted out of the water. The chocolate catfish is actually well armoured with protective spines on the leading edge of a number of its fins and over much of its body. This can make it difficult to catch these fish in a net, because they will become entangled in it; it may be better to try to drive them into a bag. Avoid handling them directly as they can draw blood.

Chocolate catfish originate from the central Amazon region and feed on a range of invertebrates, with worms of various types being especially favoured. They are rather secretive by nature and will hide away in aquarium surroundings, burying into the substrate or underneath rocks, becoming more active at dusk. The decor must be secure to prevent any injuries.

Sexing is possible on the basis of the coloration of their underparts. Males have brown and white spotting evident here, whereas female chocolate catfish are reputed to be entirely brown. Their spawn is likely to be laid in a pit on the floor of their quarters, and may be guarded by both adult fish. Hatching is likely to take place about 5 days later.

Red-tailed Catfish *(Phractocephalus hemiliopterus)*

In recent years, a number of small specimens of this catfish have been available. This species is widely distributed through the waters of the Amazon in northern South America, from Peru eastwards to Guyana and Brazil. Red-tailed catfish are unmistakable in appearance, even at this stage, with a prominent whitish-cream throat and stripes extending down the sides of the body to the red rays of the caudal fin. There may be some mottling on the dark grey upper parts, with the belly area being a similar colour.

Elegant, but predatory by nature, these catfish are really more suitable for a conservatory pond as they grow larger. In the early stages however, they will settle well in aquarium surroundings and become quite tame. Their tank must offer plenty of space for swim-

ming and it may be safer to use an external heater because, like some other larger fish, these catfish may attack aquarium equipment.

It is not possible to keep them with other fish, which are likely to be eaten. Persuading red-tailed catfish to feed on prepared foods can be difficult. They will hunt river shrimp and similar creatures with great determination. Having fed, the belly area will appear decidedly swollen and the fish is then likely to rest on the floor of the aquarium so it can digest its meal. They may sometimes eat pieces of fruit as well.

There appears to be no reliable means of sexing these fish. It has been suggested that males have a more vibrant red tail, but this could be just a regional difference. Successful spawning is not likely to take place within the confines of an aquarium in any event.

LOACHES AND ODDITIES

This section features a number of the other striking and unusual, although not necessarily rare, tropical fish which may be available on occasions. Some of these require brackish water surroundings, often being found in river estuaries close to the sea. A suitable environment can be created quite easily by adding marine salt to the aquarium water, but this will limit their choice of companions to other species requiring similar water conditions.

Ask the dealer about the concentration of salt in which the fish are being kept at the time of purchase and add the required amount to the aquarium on your return home. It is very important not to alter the concentration rapidly, because this is likely to have harmful effects on the osmoregulatory abilities of the fish and will be stressful, if not fatal, for them. The increased salinity will draw water out of their bodies, resulting in dehydration. Fish living in salt water must adapt by drinking more to counter the effects of this increased water loss. In freshwater surroundings the situation is reversed, with water passing into their bodies by osmosis and having to be excreted.

Coolie Loach *(Acanthophthalmus kuhlii)*

These eel-like fish originate from the Malay Peninsula and offshore islands such as Java and Sumatra. They are easy to maintain, especially in a well-planted tank with a sandy bottom. Bogwood arranged so that the loaches can hide in crevices, or tubular retreats fixed horizontally into the substrate, will help to make them feel secure.

Coolie loaches like to burrow, so a sandy base to their aquarium is recommended. It is important that the under-gravel filter is a snug fit across the base of the tank or the loaches may disappear beneath it and are unlikely to be seen. In a number of cases, aquarists thought their coolie loaches had died only for the fish to be rediscovered in perfect health during routine aquarium maintenance.

Feeding these loaches is straightforward. They will eat worms, but also take prepared foods quite readily on the floor of the aquarium. There are two distinct subspecies; the coolie loach itself (*A. k. kuhlii*) has up to 20 black bands on the sides of its body that do not encircle the belly. The basic body coloration can vary from yellowish-orange through to red. In contrast, the Sumatran coolie loach (*A. k. sumatranus*) tends to have fewer bands, typically less than 15, which extend lower down the sides of the body. Coloration in this case varies from golden shades of yellow to pale salmon pink.

Coolie loaches can be spawned in the aquarium and, since they should be kept in groups, pairing is not usually a problem. They entwine around each other when spawning, with their eggs being scattered in the aquarium. When attempting to catch these fish, watch for the spine present beneath each eye as this can become entangled in the net.

4in
10cm

Clown Loach *(Botia macrantha)*

This species is also sometimes called the tiger loach, because of its striped markings. Individuals may vary somewhat in their depth of coloration with some displaying a deeper shade of orange than others. The ventral and caudal fins are reddish, with the third stripe extending through part of the anal fin. Catching these fish can again be difficult because of the presence of a spine below each eye. If a loach does become caught up, it should be transferred gently and allowed to free itself so as to avoid risk of injury. This species has four pairs of sensory barbels around its mouth.

The clown loach originates from parts of Indonesia, and also occurs on Sumatra and Borneo. These fish live together in groups, but may also display territorial behaviour on occasions. Dividing the aquarium up with rocks and similar decor should avoid any risk of serious conflict.

Sexing is possible on the basis that males generally have larger caudal fins. Breeding has taken place occasionally in

12in
30cm

home aquaria, but tends not to be commonplace. Fresh, turbulent water in the spawning tank is recommended initially, so as to mimic the rain-swollen rivers which appear to trigger reproductive activity among these fish in their native habitat.

Dwarf Loach *(Botia sidthimunki)*

The unusual chain-like pattern running down the upper flanks of this fish has led to it also being known as the chained loach. There is a dark stripe beneath, running down each side of the body. Originating from Thailand, the dwarf loach is an active fish which shows to good effect in groups. It may also occur in northern India.

Unlike many loaches, which hide away for much of the day until dusk, this species is often seen swimming during the day, resting for intervals by supporting itself on its pectoral fins.

Being the smallest *Botia* species, the dwarf loach can be kept in the company of other non-aggressive fish. In their natural environment these loaches live in muddy stretches of water, so it is best to use an aquarium with a dark base. Feeding is

3in
7.5cm

straightforward, as a wide variety of foods will be readily accepted and freeze-dried items such as tubifex are often preferred.

Unfortunately, there appears to be no means of distinguishing the sexes visually and breeding in aquarium surroundings does not yet appear to have been recorded. Increasing the quantity of livefood in their diet may encourage breeding.

Zebra Loach *(Botia striata)*

Rather confusingly, these loaches are also sometimes called tiger loaches–which is the common name shared with the clown loach (*B. macrantha*). Although both have a striped pattern there is no difficulty in distinguishing between them, partly because the zebra loach is considerably smaller in size. Its basic body coloration is golden, broken with a series of black bands which create a striped appearance. Black stripes can also be seen on the fins, where they form an indistinct pattern.

Zebra loaches originate from southern India, where they are found in streams. They do not differ significantly in their requirements from other *Botia* species. A well-planted aquarium, with bogwood to provide these relatively small loaches with opportunities to hide, especially during the day, is recommended. Regular water changes are important, every 2 weeks or so, since these fish normally inhabit flowing waters where there is little likelihood of pollutants building up in the water. Livefood should feature prominently in their diet, with worms being favoured, although they will also eat formulated foods.

3in
7.5cm

Mouse Botia *(Botia horae)*

These loaches are predominantly yellowish in colour, with a distinct black band running down the back to the caudal fin. Dark markings may also be apparent on the flanks, particularly close to the caudal fin itself. Originating from parts of northern India and Thailand, this species is also known both as the skunk loach and Hora's loach. Its longitudinal stripe sets it apart from all other loaches.

A relatively soft substrate is recommended for an aquarium housing these fish, because they may burrow there. At this stage, their sandy colour and the black stripe may serve to provide them with effective camouflage. Peaceful by nature, mouse botias will hunt for worms and other food in the lower reaches of the aquarium.

As with other related species they do like to retreat under cover, and they may seek to enter under an under-gravel filtration system if there is

4in
10cm

room. The provision of suitable tubework as tank decor is therefore recommended and care should be taken also to ensure that the under-gravel filter plate covers the entire base of the tank. The digging habits of the mouse botia may sometimes result in disturbance to plants as well, but this is not usually a serious problem.

Subdued lighting is preferred by these fish, so floating plants should be included in their aquarium. Apparently, mouse botias cannot be sexed visually and they are also unlikely to be persuaded to spawn in aquarium surroundings.

Indian Glassfish *(Chanda ranga)*

This has proved to be a controversial fish in the past; its transparent appearance has led to dyes being injected into its body, providing artificial colouring in garish shades of green, purple and other colours. This cruel process is now far less commonly seen than in the past but, even so, such fish should never be purchased.

Indian glassfish are nervous fish by nature and settle best if kept in small groups. They originate not only from India but also from parts of Burma and Thailand, where they may sometimes be found in brackish as well as fresh water. Male Indian glassfish can be distinguished by the shape of their swim bladder which is pointed towards the rear, while their dorsal and anal fins have bluish borders. In contrast, females tend to be paler in terms of their overall coloration, with a more rounded swim bladder.

These fish often do better if kept in water to which marine salt has been added. Plenty of retreats, both among plants and other tank decor, should be included in their aquarium. They must be fed on livefood, in various forms, although they will eat formulated foods, notably flake.

Indian glassfish can be induced to spawn quite easily, by transferring them to a spawning tank which catches sunlight and where the water temperature is a few degrees higher, up to 82°F (28°C), than in the main aquarium. Their spawn will be deposited between plants, with each female producing as many as 150 eggs. Hatching is likely to take just a day and the fry will start to swim after a similar interval. Using brackish water for spawning can prevent the fungus attacking the eggs.

Bumblebee Goby *(Brachygobius xanthozona)*

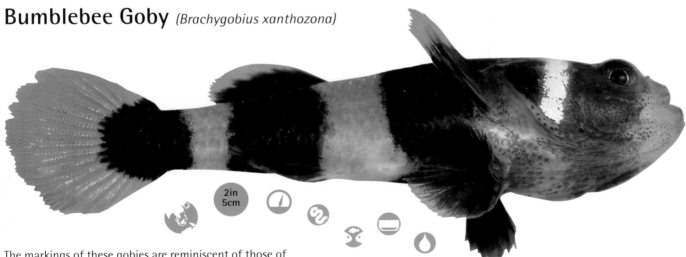

The markings of these gobies are reminiscent of those of a bumblebee, being a combination of yellow and black. Females are generally plumper and rather less colourful than males. These fish are widely distributed through south-east Asia, often being present in brackish water. Similar conditions are beneficial in aquarium surroundings, with the addition of one or two spoonfuls of sea salt per 2.5 imperial gallons (10 litres) of tank water being recommended.

Bumblebee gobies feed on livefood of all types, including mosquito larvae and whiteworm. They will spend their time on the bottom of the tank when adult, cupping their ventral fins to enable them to grip on to a surface. These gobies will prove to be highly territorial and they require plenty of retreats, such as upturned flowerpots, rocks and bogwood.

Just prior to the onset of spawning, the female bumblebee goby develops an ovipositor through which she will produce her eggs. The eggs, numbering up to 200 in total, will be concealed under a rock or in a similar secluded locality. The male watches over them until the fry hatch about 4 days later. The eggs are susceptible to fungus, particularly in fresh water.

Once the young bumblebee gobies are able to swim freely, they will occupy the middle part of the aquarium. Infusoria or a similar substitute will be needed for rearing purposes.

Four-eyed Fish *(Anableps anableps)*

These strange, surface-dwelling fish are so called because of the way in which part of their eyes protrudes above the water level. Their eyes are divided into halves, by means of a strip of the conjunctiva, with each half functioning independently. This bizarre arrangement means that while they can see possible prey in the water, they are also well placed to detect danger from above. If threatened, four-eyed fish will jump out of the water to escape rather than diving. They have flattened heads and relatively long, narrow bodies.

Four-eyed fish need to be housed in a relatively shallow aquarium with plenty of space for swimming, although plants can be set in the substrate. They are often found in brackish water and the addition of sea salt, as recommended for the bumblebee goby, will be beneficial in this case as well. Live insects, such as crickets and earthworms, can form the basis of their diet, although they will take freeze-dried foods and flake.

The male has a distinct gonopodium, which protrudes to one side. Mating must therefore occur on this side with a female which has a genital opening of the opposite configuration. They are sexually mature from 6in (15cm) long. A maximum of four offspring will be born and they will be at least 1in (2.5cm) long at this stage. They can be reared on *Daphnia* or invertebrates of a similar size, such as fruit fly, without difficulty. Mature females may breed twice each year.

Long-nosed Elephant Fish *(Gnathonemus petersi)*

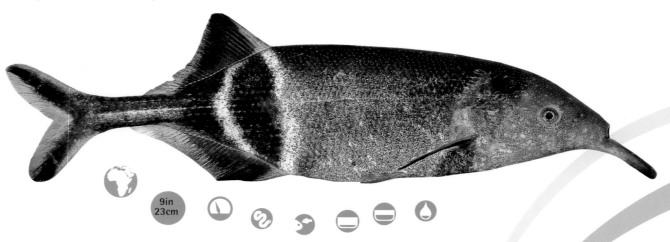

The long trunk-like proboscis of these fish explains their common name. They inhabit muddy stretches of water, probing here for worms and similar livefood. They will use their pronounced lower jaw to dig in the substrate, taking food into their mouth above. This particular species is brownish-black in colour, with distinctive yellowish-white streaks running down the body from the dorsal to the anal fin.

Long-nosed elephant fish are relatively shy by nature and, as a result, they require a well-planted aquarium with a soft substrate and subdued lighting. They will become more active at dusk and do not tolerate others of their genus, although they are not aggressive towards other fish.

Elephant fish have a large brain, which may be linked to the production of electrical impulses. These impulses help the fish to navigate in darkness, thus avoiding collisions. The electrical output of these fish has also been used to monitor water quality in Germany. When this deteriorates, the number of electrical pulsations produced by these fish increase and their behaviour changes as they swim around rather nervously. Sadly, it has not proved possible to breed the elephant-nosed fish successfully in aquaria, nor can the sexes be distinguished easily by their appearance.

Butterfly Fish *(Pantodon bucholzi)*

The wing-like structure of the pectoral fins of these fish is
responsible for their common name. They can also leap
out of their aquarium if it is not covered. The
shape of the rear of the anal fin provides a means
of separating the sexes, with this area being
straight in the case of the female butterfly fish
rather than curved as in males. Butterfly fish are
insectivorous in their feeding habits, taking a wide
variety of livefood ranging from mosquito larvae
to mini mealworms. Unfortunately, butterfly fish
may also eat smaller fish so their companions need
to be chosen with care.

A relatively shallow tank will suffice for them.
These fish will often congregate beneath floating
plants, which would naturally provide them with
cover, darting out from here to seize prey. A similar
arrangement should be provided in their aquarium.

Breeding depends firstly on conditioning the
pair with plenty of livefood. Their eggs rise to the
surface and can be scooped out easily each day, with over 200 resulting from a single spawning
over several days. At this stage the eggs will be transparent, but they soon darken and the fry will
hatch within 2 days. Tiny livefoods will be essential as a first food, but rearing can prove to be
problematical on occasions.

Spiny Eel *(Macrognathus aculeatus)*

Members of this genus all have elongated bodies and young
specimens are frequently available. It is important though to
try to determine the species on offer because some can rapidly
outgrow the average aquarium, potentially reaching lengths in
excess of 40in (100cm).

This particular species is also known as the Indian eye-spot
eel because of the characteristic eye-like spots towards the
rear of its body on the dorsal fin, of which there can be
between three and ten. It does not just occur in Indian waters
however, having a wider distribution through much of
south-east Asia.

Spiny eels occur in both fresh and brackish water and the
addition of sea salt to their aquarium water can be beneficial

as a result. They feed on livefood and represent a danger to
small fish. A sandy base to the aquarium and retreats where
these eels can curl up are recommended.

Spawning is rarely accomplished in aquaria, but females are
known to be mature by 8in (20cm) long. At this stage, they
develop an ovipositor and anal papilla, but it is otherwise
impossible to sex these fish reliably. As many as 1000 eggs will
be laid, with hatching taking 3 days. The fry, which are free-
swimming after a similar interval, can be reared successfully
on *Cyclops*.

African Knife Fish *(Xenomystus nigri)*

This species was first discovered in the Niger River in West Africa and named because of its resemblance in shape to a knife blade. Its coloration can vary from dark brown to brownish-grey, and there may sometimes be vertical stripes apparent on its body. This particular knife fish can be easily distinguished from related species since it does not have a dorsal fin.

Although it is possible to keep these knife fish in groups when they are young, they will become more territorial as they grow larger and may have to be separated at this stage. These knife fish will not disturb companions of similar size however, although they are likely to prey on small fish. A variety of livefood, such as mini mealworms, waxmoth larvae and earthworms, should form their regular diet, with smaller individuals being fed on items such as whiteworm and mosquito larvae.

Their aquarium must include well-planted areas and clear stretches enabling these fish to swim, especially at night when they become more active. African knife fish occasionally utter bell-like sounds as air is ejected from their swim bladder. Their breeding requirements are not well understood, although females have been known to lay up to 200 eggs in a single spawning. The body coloration of these fish assumes a more purplish hue at this stage, becoming reddish-brown in some instances.

12in
30cm

South American Leaf Fish *(Monocirrhus polyacanthus)*

Resembling a dead leaf drifting in the water provides these fish with an ability to seize prey largely undetected. South American leaf fish vary from shades of yellow through to dark brown, blending in with their habitat. They often hide in among plants with their head pointing slightly downwards in the water.

Unfortunately, these fish are not always easy to maintain, with water conditions proving critical. It is a good idea to filter the water through peat. They must not be kept with smaller fish as these are likely to be eaten. In some cases however, young guppies may be needed to persuade South American leaf fish to eat; mosquito larvae are also eaten readily.

Females are generally slightly larger than males and will deposit their spawn on to rockwork or other surfaces in the tank, with the chosen site being cleaned beforehand. As many as 300 eggs will be laid, with the male then guarding the eggs until they hatch about 4 days later. Foods such as *Cyclops* can be given once they are free-swimming. As the young leaf fish grow they should be separated into groups comprising individuals of similar size, to prevent the risk of cannibalism.

4in
10cm

Dwarf Rainbowfish *(Melanotaenia maccullochi)*

These attractive fish originate from southern Papua and New Guinea as well as northern Australia, where they occur as far south as Sydney. Males can be distinguished by their longer dorsal and anal fins, and their colouring is also more pronounced. This species is sometimes described as the black-lined rainbowfish, as dark markings are apparent on the flanks.

Their care is straightforward and breeding is quite feasible. Livefood such as *Daphnia* is vital for spawning purposes. The eggs will be laid in fine-leaved plants such as *Myriophyllum*. A female may produce as many as 200 eggs, which will be attached to the plants by threads. It is important to keep the eggs in darkened surroundings until they hatch about a week later. The adult fish should be removed after spawning because they are likely to eat their eggs. Transferring them elsewhere also lessens the pollution in the spawning tank. The young can be reared without difficulty on a suitable fry food.

Celebes Rainbowfish *(Telmatherina ladigesi)*

The delicate coloration of these fish is influenced by their environment and, depending on the lighting, they can be brighter. There is a pale bluish-green area running down the midline, with the body having a yellowish hue overall. Celebes rainbowfish have two dorsal fins with the second one being considerably elongated, particularly in the case of the male. The anal fin is similarly enlarged and is a combination of black and yellow in colour.

The distribution of this species is centred on the island of Sulawesi (formerly Celebes). These fish can be kept with other non-aggressive species which will not damage their elongated fins. They are relatively undemanding in terms of watr chemistry and may be kept satisfactorily in hard water. It may be helpful to add some marine salt however, to create a brackish environment for them.

Celebes rainbowfish feed on algae; if this is not available other plant foods such as spinach should be offered. Livefoods are also important. Spawning can take place in a well-planted aquarium, with the female laying her large eggs here. It will be safer to remove the adult fish at this stage, so there is no risk of the eggs being eaten.

Green Pufferfish *(Tetraodon fluviatilis)*

Many pufferfish are marine species, but this particular species occurs in both fresh and brackish waters. Most aquarists add a little sea salt to a tank housing this species. Green pufferfish will not usually spawn readily in fresh water, although neither will they survive in a marine aquarium. These fish have a wide distribution, from India eastwards through much of south-east Asia as far as the Philippines.

Green pufferfish can be distinguished by their yellowish-green coloration, broken by dark brownish spots and blotches. Watch for individuals that keep their tail curved round the side of the body as this is a sign of ill health, as is the appearance of black areas on their normally white belly. These fish may be combined with companions of similar size, but they tend to be quarrelsome among themselves. Plants set around the sides and back of the tank may help to avoid serious conflict by providing suitable retreats.

In time, green pufferfish can become very tame. They are also potentially long-lived, with a life expectancy of at least nine years in aquarium surroundings. Their diet is important. It must include hard-shelled items such as snails, in order to wear down their teeth. If these become overgrown the pufferfish will not be able to eat and unless they are clipped back, it will die of starvation. Livefood form the bulk of their diet, but they may also eat formulated foods such as tablets.

The female will spawn on rockwork, laying up to 300 eggs which are then watched over by the male even for a period after they hatch. This will take about a day or so, with the fry subsequently feeding on brine shrimp *nauplii*, rotifers and similar foods.

Mono *(Monodactylus argenteus)*

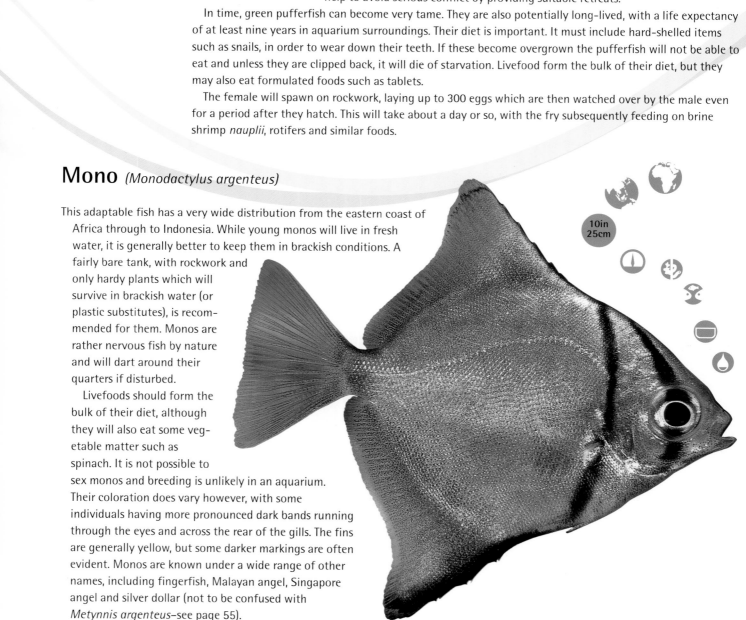

This adaptable fish has a very wide distribution from the eastern coast of Africa through to Indonesia. While young monos will live in fresh water, it is generally better to keep them in brackish conditions. A fairly bare tank, with rockwork and only hardy plants which will survive in brackish water (or plastic substitutes), is recommended for them. Monos are rather nervous fish by nature and will dart around their quarters if disturbed.

Livefoods should form the bulk of their diet, although they will also eat some vegetable matter such as spinach. It is not possible to sex monos and breeding is unlikely in an aquarium. Their coloration does vary however, with some individuals having more pronounced dark bands running through the eyes and across the rear of the gills. The fins are generally yellow, but some darker markings are often evident. Monos are known under a wide range of other names, including fingerfish, Malayan angel, Singapore angel and silver dollar (not to be confused with *Metynnis argenteus*–see page 55).

Tiger Scat *(Scatophagus argus)*

Another fish which thrives in brackish water, the tiger scat is omnivorous in its feeding habits. It is therefore best kept in an aquarium decorated with plastic plants, because these fish are liable to destroy any vegetation in their quarters. They can be fed a selection of vegetarian foods, including spinach and rolled oats.

Tiger scats are widely distributed; older individuals prefer more brackish surroundings and often venture out from estuaries into the open sea in the wild. They can be kept satisfactorily with other fish which require a similar environment, such as the mono, but always check on the water conditions which these and other brackish water fish have been used to at the time of purchase.

Aim to replicate these surroundings at first, to enable the fish to adjust to the move with minimum stress, and then introduce changes gradually by making the water more brackish over successive water changes. If kept in fresh water alone, scats are more likely to succumb to fungus. They can become quite tame, but breeding has not yet been achieved in the home aquarium.

12in
30cm

Arowana *(Osteoglossum bicirrhosum)*

47in
120cm

The arowana is a representative of an ancient group called bony-tongued fish, as reflected in their scientific name of *Osteoglossum*. A fish of great significance in the Far East, where large specimens are highly prized, the arowana occurs naturally in the flood plains of the Amazon. These are highly predatory fish by nature, and should be kept on their own, particularly as they grow larger.

Plants and tank decor must be situated so as to give the arowana space for swimming. These fish often spend periods of time close to the surface and may breathe air directly via their swim bladders. Male arowanas can be distinguished by their longer anal fin and more pronounced lower jaw. The male is responsible for brooding the eggs in his mouth after spawning occurs, using aspecial pouch for this purpose located in the bones of the jaw. The eggs hatch after a period of about 2 months, with the fry being up to 4in (10cm) long by this stage and capable of taking larger livefoods without difficulty.

GLOSSARY

Acid–a reading on the pH scale of a water sample giving a figure below 7.

Adipose fin–a small fin located between the dorsal and caudal fin on the back. Its function is unclear and it is not present in all fish.

Alkaline–a reading on the pH scale of a water sample which results in a figure above 7.

Anal fin–the unpaired fin close to the vent on the underside of the fish's body.

Barbels–fleshy projections located around the mouth which have a sensory function in assisting fish, typically those living in murky water, to locate their food.

Brackish–water conditions reflecting a mixture of salt and freshwater. These conditions typically occur in estuaries.

Brine shrimp *nauplii*–the larval form of the brine shrimp, used as a rearing food for many tropical fish in aquarium surroundings.

Bubble nest–the saliva structure built by many species of male labyrinth fish at the surface of the water, and often attached to the plants there, where their eggs will be kept until hatching.

Caudal fin–also known as the tail fin, it is responsible for providing the main propulsive thrust for the fish as it swims.

Dorsal fin–the fin located in the mid-line on the upper part of the fish's back. It can provide a means of distinguishing the sexes in some cases.

Egg layer–a fish which reproduces by means of passing its eggs into the external environment before the young emerge.

Egg spots–characteristic brightly coloured ovoid spots on the anal fin of male mouth-brooding cichlids.

Family–a group of fish comprising a number of different genera.

Fancy–a strain of fish which has been selectively bred for its decorative value.

Free-swimming–the stage at which young fish can start to swim freely in search of their own food, having used up their yolk sac reserves.

Fry–young fish.

Genus–a group containing one or more species of fish. The plural form is genera.

Gills–structures located behind the head, richly endowed with blood vessels, which allow the fish to extract oxygen from the water passing through them.

Gonopodium–the elongated, grooved anal fin of male livebearers used to inseminate the female.

Gravid–the characteristic swollen appearance of the female fish prior to giving birth or laying eggs.

Hard water–a reflection of the presence of dissolved calcium or magnesium salts in water, measured in the degrees dH scale. A reading above 12°dH indicates increasing hardness.

Labyrinth organ–a characteristic feature of the labyrinth fish, located close to the gills, which enables this group of fish to breathe atmospheric air directly.

Lateral line–sensory mechanism running down each side of the body allowing fish to detect vibrations in the water near them.

Length–fish are typically measured from the snout to the base of the caudal fin; the length of the caudal fin itself is excluded.

Livebearer–a fish which reproduces by means of eggs that are fertilized internally; the eggs are retained inside the fish's body until they are due to hatch.

Morph–a colour variant within a species which is known to occur in the wild. Often encountered in the case of Rift Valley cichlids.

Mouth-brooder–a fish which retains its fertilized eggs in its mouth until they hatch.

Mulm–the detritus made up of plant matter, fish waste and other material, which can accumulate on the floor of the aquarium.

Nuchal hump–the swelling seen on the head of a number of mature male cichlids.

Operculum–the flap which serves to cover the gills, located behind the eyes on each side of the head.

Pectoral fins–the pair of small fins on each side of the body behind the gills.

Pelvic fins–the two fins that are located in front of the anal fin, on the lower part of the fish's body.

Pharyngeal teeth–teeth-like projections present in the throat of cyprinids.

Rays–the vertical bony projections which provide structural support for the fins.

Salt mix–specially formulated products to re-create specific water conditions such as brackish water.

Scale–the protective covering that is present on the bodies of most fish.

Shoal–a group of fish swimming together, usually of the same species.

Soft water–water which lacks dissolved mineral salts, such as pure rainwater, often measured on the degrees dH scale. A reading below 6°dH indicates increasing softness.

Spawning–the process of egg laying and mating.

Species–a category of fish which closely resemble each other and will freely interbreed with one another to produce fertile offspring.

Strain–a particular lineage of fish, selected and bred for a specific feature such as colour or fin shape.

Subspecies–a division of the species category, often the result of isolated populations giving rise to slight local variance in coloration.

Substrate–the floor covering, typically gravel or sand, used in the aquarium.

Swim bladder–the buoyancy aid used by most fish to enable them to maintain their position in the water.

Tubercles–slight swellings on the fins or body, which may indicate the sex of cyprinids or could indicate ill health.

Vent–the ano-genital orifice of the fish.

Yolk sac–the means by which the young of egg laying fish are nourished until they eventually become free-swimming and begin to seek their own food sources.

BIBLIOGRAPHY

Alderton, David. *Looking after Freshwater Aquarium Fish.* Ward Lock (1983); Blandford Press (1995).

Andrews, Chris. *A Fishkeeper's Guide to Fish Breeding.* Salamander Books (1986).

Andrews, Chris; Exell, A. and Carrington, Neville. *The Manual of Fish Health.* Salamander Books (1988).

Axelrod, Herbert R.; Burgess, Warren E.; Pronek, Neal and Walls, Jerry G. *Dr. Axelrod's Atlas of Freshwater Aquarium Fishes.* T.F.H. Publications (1985)

Axelrod, Herbert R. and Wischnath, L. *Swordtails and Platies.* T.F.H. Publications (1991).

Bailey, Mary and Sandford, Gina. *The Ultimate Aquarium.* Lorenz Books (1995).

Burgess, Warren E. *An Atlas of Freshwater and Marine Catfishes.* T.F.H. Publications (1989)

Dawes, John. *Livebearing Fishes.* Blandford Press (1991).

Ferraris, Carl. *Catfish in the Aquarium.* Tetra Press (1991).

Iwaski, Noboru. *Guppies–Fancy Strains and How to Produce Them.* T.F.H. Publications (1989).

James, Barry. *A Fishkeeper's Guide to Aquarium Plants.* Salamander Books (1986).

Linke, Horst. *Labyrinth Fish–The Bubble-Nest Builders.* Tetra Press (1991)

Linke, Horst and Staeck, Wolfgang. *American Cichlids 1: Dwarf Cichlids.* Tetra Press (1994).

Linke, Horst and Staeck, Wolfgang. *American Cichlids 2: Large Cichlids.* Tetra Press (1994).

Linke, Horst and Staeck, Wolfgang. *African Cichlids 1: Cichlids from West Africa.* Tetra Press (1994).

Linke, Horst and Staeck, Wolfgang. *African Cichlids 2: Cichlids from Eastern Africa.* Tetra Press (1994).

Loiselle, Paul V. *A Fishkeeper's Guide to African Cichlids.* Salamander Books (1988).

Richter, Hans-Joachim. *Gouramis and other Anabantoids.* T.F.H. Publications (1988).

Riehl, R. and Baensch, Hans. *Baensch Aquarium Atlas.* Baensch (1987).

Sands, David. *A Fishkeeper's Guide to African and Asian Catfishes.* Salamander Books (1986).

Sands, David. *A Fishkeeper's Guide to South American Catfishes.* Salamander Books (1988).

Scheel, Jorgen J. *Atlas of Killifishes of the Old World.* T.F.H. Publications (1990).

Schmidt-Focke, Eduard. *Eduard Schmidt-Focke's Discus Book.* T.F.H. Publications (1990).

Scott, Peter W. *A Fishkeeper's Guide to Livebearing Fishes.* Salamander Books (1987).

Sterba, G. and Mills, Dick (eds). *The Aquarist's Encyclopaedia.* Blandford Press (1983).

Vierke, Jörg. *Bettas, Gouramis and other Anabantoids: Labyrinth Fishes of the World.* T.F.H. Publications (1988).

Ward, Brian. *The Aquarium Fish Survival Manual.* Macdonald (1985).

INDEX

ACKNOWLEDGEMENTS

The Publishers would like to thank the following sources for their kind permission to reproduce the photographs in this book:

KEY: b=bottom, c=centre, l=left, r=right, t=top

Bruce Coleman Ltd/Jane Burton 18bl, 18br, 58, /Hans Reinhard 11tl;

Reed International Books Ltd /Paul Forrester 4, 5, 6, 7tl, 7tr, 7b, 10cl, 10cr, 10/11b, 11tr, 11cl, 11cr, 12tr, 12tl, 12br, 12bl, 13t, 13c, 13bl, 13br, 14cl, 14c, 14cr, 14b, 15tr, 15tl, 15c, 16t, 16c, 17, 20t;

Photomax 1t, 1b, 2/3, 15b, 20cb, 21b, 22, 23t, 23b, 24t, 24b, 25t, 25b, 26t, 26b, 27b, 28t, 28b, 29t, 29b, 30t, 30b, 31t, 31b, 32t, 32b, 33t, 34t, 34b, 35t, 35b, 36t, 36b, 37, 38t, 38b, 39t, 39b, 40t, 40b, 41t, 41b, 42t, 42b, 43t, 43b, 44t, 44b, 45t, 45b, 46t, 47t, 47b, 48t, 48b, 49t, 49b, 50t, 50b, 51t, 51b, 52t, 52b, 53t, 53b, 54t, 54b, 55t, 55b, 56t, 57t, 57b, 59t, 59b, 60t, 60b, 61t, 61b, 62t, 62b, 63t, 63b, 64t, 64b, 65t, 65b, 66t, 66b, 67t, 67b, 68t, 69t, 70t, 70b, 71t, 71b, 72t, 73t, 73b, 74t, 74b, 75t, 75b, 76t, 77, 78t, 78b, 79t, 79b, 80t, 80b, 81t, 81b, 82t, 82b, 83t, 83b, 84t, 84b, 85, 86t, 86b, 87t, 88t, 88b, 89t, 90t, 90b, 91t, 91b, 92t, 92b, 94, 95t, 95b, 96t, 96b, 97b, 97t, 97b, 98b, 99t, 99b, 100, 101t, 101b, 102t, 102b, 103t, 103b, 104t, 104b, 105t, 105b, 106t, 106b, 107t, 108t, 108b, 109t, 109b, 110t, 110b, 111t, 111b, 112t, 112b, 113t, 113b, 114, 115t, 115b, 116t, 116b, 117t, 117b, 118t, 118b, 119t, 119b, 120t, 120b, 121t, 121b, 122t, 122b, 123t, 123b;

Arend van den Nieuwenhuizen 69b;

M. Sandford 19tl, 19tr, 20bl, 20br, 27t, 68b;

TFH Publications 56b, 72b, 76b, 93b, /Dr Herbert R. Axelrod 107b, /Dr Karl Knaack 87b, 93t, /Hans-Joachim Richter 33b, 46b, 89b, 98t.